NIGHT

Elie Weisel

EDITORIAL DIRECTOR Justin Kestler
MANAGING EDITOR Ben Florman

SERIES EDITORS Boomie Aglietti, Justin Kestler
PRODUCTION Christian Lorentzen

WRITERS Josh Perry, Jon Natchez
EDITORS Benjamin Morgan, Sarah Friedberg

This edition published by Spark Publishing

Spark Publishing
A Division of SparkNotes LLC
120 Fifth Avenue, 8th Floor
New York, NY 10011

02 03 04 05 SN 9 8 7 6 5 4 3 2 1

Please send all comments and questions or report errors to
feedback@sparknotes.com.

Library of Congress information available upon request

Printed and bound in the United States

RRD-C

ISBN 1-58663-398-8

INTRODUCTION: STOPPING TO BUY SPARKNOTES ON A SNOWY EVENING

Whose words these are you *think* you know.
Your paper's due tomorrow, though;
We're glad to see you stopping here
To get some help before you go.

Lost your course? You'll find it here.
Face tests and essays without fear.
Between the words, good grades at stake:
Get great results throughout the year.

Once school bells caused your heart to quake
As teachers circled each mistake.
Use SparkNotes and no longer weep,
Ace every single test you take.

Yes, books are lovely, dark, and deep,
But only what you grasp you keep,
With hours to go before you sleep,
With hours to go before you sleep.

Contents

NOTE: This SparkNote refers to the 1989 Bantam Books edition of *Night,* translated from the French by Stella Rodway, featuring a foreword by François Mauriac, and a preface by Robert McAfee Brown. As the Rodway translation is standard, there is no variation between English editions of the text.

CONTEXT

ELIE WIESEL WAS BORN on September 30, 1928, in Sighet, a small town in Transylvania that was then part of Romania but became part of Hungary in 1940. Wiesel's Orthodox Jewish family was highly observant of Jewish tradition. His father, Shlomo, a shopkeeper, was very involved with the Jewish community, which was confined to the Jewish section of town, called the shtetl. As a child and teenager, Wiesel distinguished himself in the study of traditional Jewish texts: the Torah (the first five books of the Old Testament), the Talmud (codified oral law), and even—unusual for someone so young—the mystical texts of the Cabbala.

Until 1944, the Jews of Hungary were relatively unaffected by the catastrophe that was destroying the Jewish communities of Europe. The leader of the German National Socialist (Nazi) party, Adolf Hitler, came to power in 1933, behind campaign rhetoric that blamed the Jews for Germany's depression after World War I. Germany embraced Hitler's argument for the superiority of the Nordic peoples, which he (mistakenly) called the Aryan race. The country soon implemented a set of laws—including the infamous Nuremberg Laws of 1935—designed to dehumanize German Jews and subject them to violence and prejudice.

As World War II progressed, Hitler and his counselors developed the "Final Solution" to the so-called Jewish Question—a program of systematic extermination of Europe's Jews. By the time the Allies defeated Germany in 1945, the Final Solution had resulted in the greatest act of genocide known to the world. Six million European Jews had been murdered, along with millions of Gypsies, homosexuals, and others whom the Nazis considered undesirable. The greatest numbers of victims were killed in concentration camps, in which Jews—and other enemies of Germany—were gathered, imprisoned, forced into labor, and, when they could no longer be of use to their captors, annihilated. In addition to the slaughter at the camps, millions of soldiers were killed in battle. By the end of World War II, more than thirty-five million people had died, over half of them civilians.

While anti-Jewish legislation was a common phenomenon in Hungary, the Holocaust itself did not reach Hungary until 1944. In

March of 1944, however, the German army occupied Hungary, installing a puppet government (a regime that depends not on the support of its citizenry but on the support of a foreign government) under Nazi control. Adolf Eichmann, the executioner of the Final Solution, came to Hungary to oversee personally the destruction of Hungary's Jews. The Nazis operated with remarkable speed: in the spring of 1944, the Hungarian Jewish community, the only remaining large Jewish community in continental Europe, was deported to concentration camps in Germany and Poland. Eventually, the Nazis murdered 560,000 Hungarian Jews, the overwhelming majority of the prewar Jewish population in Hungary. In Wiesel's native Sighet, the disaster was even worse: of the 15,000 Jews in prewar Sighet, only about fifty families survived the Holocaust. In May of 1944, when Wiesel was fifteen, his family and many inhabitants of the Sighet shtetl were deported to the Auschwitz concentration camp in Poland. The largest and deadliest of the camps, Auschwitz was the site of more than 1,300,000 Jewish deaths. Wiesel's father, mother, and little sister all died in the Holocaust. Wiesel himself survived and emigrated to France.

After observing a ten-year vow of silence about the Holocaust, in 1956 Wiesel published *Un di Velt Hot Geshvign* (Yiddish for *And the World Remained Silent*), an 800-page account of his life during the Holocaust. In 1958, he condensed his work and translated it from its original Yiddish into French, publishing it under the title *La Nuit*. The work was translated into English and published in 1960 as *Night*. Some scholars have argued that significant differences exist between *Un di Velt Hot Geshvign* and the subsequent French/English publications, chiefly that in the Yiddish text, Wiesel expressed more anger toward the Nazis and adopted a more vengeful tone.

Although publishers were initially hesitant to embrace *Night,* believing that audiences would not be interested in such pessimistic subject matter, the memoir now stands as one of the most widely read and taught accounts of the Holocaust. From a literary point of view, it opened the way for many other stories and memoirs published in the second half of the twentieth century. In 1963, Wiesel became an American citizen; he now lives in New York City.

NIGHT AS A LITERARY WORK

While *Night* is Elie Wiesel's testimony about his experiences in the Holocaust, Wiesel is not, precisely speaking, the story's protagonist. *Night* is narrated by a boy named Eliezer who represents Wiesel, but details differentiate the character Eliezer from the real-life Wiesel. For instance, Eliezer wounds his foot in the concentration camps, while Wiesel wounded his knee.

Wiesel fictionalizes seemingly unimportant details because he wants to distinguish his narrator from himself. It is almost impossibly painful for a survivor to write about his Holocaust experience, and the mechanism of a narrator allows Wiesel to distance himself somewhat from the experience, to look in from the outside. Also, Wiesel is interested in documenting emotional truth as well as the historical truth about physical events. *Night* is the story of a boy who survives the concentration camps, but it also traces Eliezer's emotional journey from a believing Orthodox Jewish boy to a profoundly disenchanted young man who questions the existence of God and, by extension, the humanity of man. Wiesel terms *Night* a "deposition"—an exact rendering of the facts as they occurred to him. But *Night* is neither a record of facts nor an impartial document. Instead, it is an attempt to re-create the thoughts and experiences that Wiesel had as a teenage concentration camp prisoner.

Because *Night*'s protagonist closely resembles its author, it may be considered more of a memoir than a novel. Nevertheless, since Wiesel employs various literary devices to make his story effective, it is important to examine how his techniques are different from those used in a novel. One important difference is that a novel typically concerns itself with creating a convincing fictional story, explaining the causes and effects of everything that occurs within its fictional world, tying up loose ends, and fleshing out all of its characters. *Night*, however, is concerned solely with Wiesel's personal experience. Whatever events lie outside the narrator's direct observation vanish from the work's perspective. After Eliezer is separated from his mother and sister, for example, he never speaks about them again, and we never learn their fate. *Night* also has other literary elements. The narrator's chance encounter in the Métro with a French woman he had known while working in the concentration camps is an encounter that usually occurs in fiction. And carefully chosen poetic language reinforces detail throughout the work. *Night*'s literary qualities, particularly the limited perspective of a first-person narrator, give us a subjective, deeply personal impression of the horrors of the Holocaust.

PLOT OVERVIEW

NOTE: *Although* Night *is not necessarily a memoir, this SparkNote often refers to it as one, since the work's mixture of testimony, deposition, and emotional truth-telling renders it similar to works in the memoir genre. It is clear that Eliezer is meant to serve, to a great extent, as author Elie Wiesel's stand-in and representative. Minor details have been altered, but what happens to Eliezer is what happened to Wiesel himself during the Holocaust. It is important to remember, however, that there is a difference between the persona of* Night's *narrator, Eliezer, and that of* Night's *author, Elie Wiesel.*

Night is narrated by Eliezer, a Jewish teenager who, when the memoir begins, lives in his hometown of Sighet, in Hungarian Transylvania. Eliezer studies the Torah (the first five books of the Old Testament) and the Cabbala (a doctrine of Jewish mysticism). His instruction is cut short, however, when his teacher, Moshe the Beadle, is deported. In a few months, Moshe returns, telling a horrifying tale: the Gestapo (the German secret police force) took charge of his train, led everyone into the woods, and systematically butchered them. Nobody believes Moshe, who is taken for a lunatic.

In the spring of 1944, the Nazis occupy Hungary. Not long afterward, a series of increasingly repressive measures are passed, and the Jews of Eliezer's town are forced into small ghettos within Sighet. Soon they are herded onto cattle cars, and a nightmarish journey ensues. After days and nights crammed into the car, exhausted and near starvation, the passengers arrive at Birkenau, the gateway to Auschwitz.

Upon his arrival in Birkenau, Eliezer and his father are separated from his mother and sisters, whom they never see again. In the first of many "selections" that Eliezer describes in the memoir, the Jews are evaluated to determine whether they should be killed immediately or put to work. Eliezer and his father seem to pass the evaluation, but before they are brought to the prisoners' barracks, they stumble upon the open-pit furnaces where the Nazis are burning babies by the truckload.

The Jewish arrivals are stripped, shaved, disinfected, and treated with almost unimaginable cruelty. Eventually, their captors march them from Birkenau to the main camp, Auschwitz. They eventually arrive in Buna, a work camp, where Eliezer is put to work in an electrical-fittings factory. Under slave-labor conditions, severely malnourished and decimated by the frequent "selections," the Jews take solace in caring for each other, in religion, and in Zionism, a movement favoring the establishment of a Jewish state in Palestine, considered the holy land. In the camp, the Jews are subject to beatings and repeated humiliations. A vicious foreman forces Eliezer to give him his gold tooth, which is pried out of his mouth with a rusty spoon.

The prisoners are forced to watch the hanging of fellow prisoners in the camp courtyard. On one occasion, the Gestapo even hang a small child who had been associated with some rebels within Buna. Because of the horrific conditions in the camps and the ever-present danger of death, many of the prisoners themselves begin to slide into cruelty, concerned only with personal survival. Sons begin to abandon and abuse their fathers. Eliezer himself begins to lose his humanity and his faith, both in God and in the people around him.

After months in the camp, Eliezer undergoes an operation for a foot injury. While he is in the infirmary, however, the Nazis decide to evacuate the camp because the Russians are advancing and are on the verge of liberating Buna. In the middle of a snowstorm, the prisoners begin a death march: they are forced to run for more than fifty miles to the Gleiwitz concentration camp. Many die of exposure to the harsh weather and exhaustion. At Gleiwitz, the prisoners are herded into cattle cars once again. They begin another deadly journey: one hundred Jews board the car, but only twelve remain alive when the train reaches the concentration camp Buchenwald. Throughout the ordeal, Eliezer and his father help each other to survive by means of mutual support and concern. In Buchenwald, however, Eliezer's father dies of dysentery and physical abuse. Eliezer survives, an empty shell of a man until April 11, 1945, the day that the American army liberates the camp.

CHARACTER LIST

Eliezer   The narrator of *Night* and the stand-in for the memoir's author, Elie Wiesel. *Night* traces Eliezer's psychological journey, as the Holocaust robs him of his faith in God and exposes him to the deepest inhumanity of which man is capable. Despite many tests of his humanity, however, Eliezer maintains his devotion to his father. It is important to note that we learn Eliezer's last name only in passing, and that it is never repeated. His story—which parallels Wiesel's own biography—is intensely personal, but it is also representative of the experiences of hundreds of thousands of Jewish teenagers.

Chlomo   Even though he is the only character other than Eliezer who is present throughout the memoir, Eliezer's father is named only once, at the end of *Night*. Chlomo is respected by the entire Jewish community of Sighet, and by his son as well. He and Eliezer desperately try to remain together throughout their concentration camp ordeal.

Moshe the Beadle   Eliezer's teacher of Jewish mysticism, Moshe is a poor Jew who lives in Sighet. He is deported before the rest of the Sighet Jews but escapes and returns to tell the town what the Nazis are doing to the Jews. Tragically, the community takes Moshe for a lunatic.

Akiba Drumer   A Jewish Holocaust victim who gradually loses his faith in God as a result of his experiences in the concentration camp.

Madame Schächter A Jewish woman from Sighet who is deported in the same cattle car as Eliezer. Madame Schächter is taken for a madwoman when, every night, she screams that she sees furnaces in the distance. She proves to be a prophetess, however, as the trains soon arrive at the crematoria of Auschwitz.

Juliek A young musician whom Eliezer meets in Auschwitz. Juliek reappears late in the memoir, when Eliezer hears him playing the violin after the death march to Gleiwitz.

Tibi and Yosi Two brothers with whom Eliezer becomes friendly in Buna. Tibi and Yosi are Zionists. Along with Eliezer, they make a plan to move to Palestine after the war.

Dr. Josef Mengele When he arrives at Auschwitz, Eliezer encounters the historically infamous Dr. Mengele. Mengele was the cruel doctor who presided over the selection of arrivals at Auschwitz/Birkenau. Known as the "Angel of Death," Mengele's words sentenced countless prisoners to death in the gas chambers. He also directed horrific experiments on human subjects at the camp.

Idek Eliezer's Kapo (a prisoner conscripted by the Nazis to police other prisoners) at the electrical equipment warehouse in Buna. Despite the fact that they also faced the cruelty of the Nazis, many Kapos were as cruel to the prisoners as the Germans. During moments of insane rage, Idek beats Eliezer.

Franek Eliezer's foreman at Buna. Franek notices Eliezer's gold tooth and gets a dentist in the camp to pry it out with a rusty spoon.

Rabbi Eliahou A devout Jewish prisoner whose son abandons him in one of many instances in *Night* of a son behaving cruelly toward his father. Eliezer prays that he will never behave as Rabbi Eliahou's son behaves.

Zalman   One of Eliezer's fellow prisoners. Zalman is trampled to death during the run to Gleiwitz.

Meir Katz Eliezer's father's friend from Buna. In the cattle car to Buchenwald, Katz saves Eliezer's life from an unidentified assailant.

Stein   Eliezer's relative from Antwerp, Belgium, whom he and his father encounter in Auschwitz. Trying to bolster his spirit, Eliezer's father lies to Stein and tells him that his family is still alive and healthy.

Hilda   Eliezer's oldest sister.

Béa   Eliezer's middle sister.

Tzipora Eliezer's youngest sister.

ANALYSIS OF MAJOR CHARACTERS

ELIEZER

Eliezer is more than just a traditional protagonist; his direct experience is the entire substance of *Night*. He tells his story in a highly subjective, first-person, autobiographical voice, and, as a result, we get an intimate, personal account of the Holocaust through direct descriptive language. Whereas many books about the Holocaust use a generalized historical or epic perspective to paint a broad picture of the period, Eliezer's account is limited in scope but gives a personal perspective through which the reader receives a harrowingly intimate description of life under the Nazis.

First and foremost, it is important to differentiate between the author of *Night*, Elie Wiesel, and its narrator and protagonist, Eliezer. That a distinction can be made does not mean that *Night* is a work of fiction. Indeed, except for minor details, what happens to Eliezer is exactly what happened to Wiesel during the Holocaust. But Wiesel alters minor details (for example, Wiesel wounded his knee in the concentration camps, while Eliezer wounds his foot) in order to place some distance, however small, between himself and his protagonist. It is extremely painful for a survivor to remember and write about his or her Holocaust experience; creating a narrator allows Wiesel to distance himself somewhat from the trauma and suffering about which he writes.

Wiesel did not write *Night* merely to document historical truths about physical events. The memoir is concerned with the emotional truth about the Holocaust, as experienced by individuals. As Eliezer struggles for survival, his most fundamental beliefs—his faith in God, faith in his fellow human beings, and sense of justice in the world—are called into question. He emerges from his experience profoundly changed. The Holocaust shakes his faith in God and the world around him, and he sees the depths of cruelty and selfishness to which any human being—including himself—can sink. Through Eliezer, Wiesel intimately conveys his horrible experiences and his transformation as a prisoner during the Holocaust.

ELIEZER'S FATHER

Aside from Eliezer, Eliezer's father, Chlomo, is the only other constant presence in the work. However, whereas Eliezer develops throughout the work, experiencing horrible revelations and undergoing numerous changes, Eliezer's father remains a fairly static character, an older man who loves his son and depends upon him for support. We do not get to hear Chlomo's thoughts about his experiences, and the only development we are shown is his gradual decline, a decline that all of the camp's prisoners experience.

This lack of insight into Chlomo reflects the work's commitment to Eliezer's perspective. Instead of understanding Chlomo and his experience objectively or through his own eyes, we see him through Eliezer's eyes. Eliezer is constantly thinking of his father, and their relationship is crucial to Eliezer's experience. Eliezer's father serves not so much as a three-dimensional character but as an aspect of Eliezer's life. We do not see what is going on in Chlomo's mind because Eliezer can tell us only about his own experience.

Chlomo is a central presence in the memoir because he is of utmost importance to Eliezer. He functions almost as the center of Eliezer's struggle for survival. Eliezer's relationship with his father reminds him of fundamental feelings of love, duty, and commitment to his family. His commitment to his father also reminds him of his own humanity, of the goodness left in his heart. All around him, he sees fellow prisoners descending to the deepest depths of selfishness and cruelty, but his relationship to his father reminds him that there is life outside of the Holocaust, and a set of fundamental moral values that transcends the cruelty and hatred of the Nazi universe.

MOSHE THE BEADLE

Moshe the Beadle is the first character introduced in *Night,* and his values resonate throughout the text, even though he himself disappears after the first few pages. Moshe represents, first and foremost, an earnest commitment to Judaism, and to Jewish mysticism in particular. As Eliezer's Cabbala teacher, Moshe talks about the riddles of the universe and God's centrality to the quest for understanding. Moshe's words frame the conflict of Eliezer's struggle for faith, which is at the center of *Night.*

In his statement "I pray to the God within me that He will give me the strength to ask Him the right questions," Moshe conveys two concepts key to Eliezer's struggle: the idea that God is everywhere, even within every individual, and the idea that faith is based on *questions,* not answers. Eliezer's struggle with faith is, for the most part, a struggle of questions. He continually asks where God has gone and questions how such evil could exist in the world. Moshe's statement tells us that these moments do not reflect Eliezer's loss of faith; instead they demonstrate his ongoing spiritual commitment. But we also see that at the lowest points of Eliezer's faith—particularly when he sees the *pipel* (a youth) hung in Buna— he is full of *answers,* not questions. At these moments, he has indeed lost the spirit of faith he learned from Moshe, and is truly faithless.

Finally, Moshe may also serve as a stand-in for Wiesel himself, as his presence evokes an overarching purpose of the entire work. As has been stated previously, *Night* can be read as an attack against silence. So many times in the work, evil is perpetuated by a silent lack of resistance or—as in the case of Moshe's warnings—by ignoring reports of evil. With *Night,* Wiesel, like Moshe, bears witness to tragedy in order to warn others, to prevent anything like the Holocaust from ever happening again.

CHARACTER ANALYSIS

Themes, Motifs & Symbols

Themes

Themes are the fundamental and often universal ideas explored in a literary work.

ELIEZER'S STRUGGLE TO MAINTAIN FAITH IN A BENEVOLENT GOD

Eliezer's struggle with his faith is a dominant conflict in *Night*. At the beginning of the work, his faith in God is absolute. When asked why he prays to God, he answers, "Why did I pray? . . . Why did I live? Why did I breathe?" His belief in an omnipotent, benevolent God is unconditional, and he cannot imagine living without faith in a divine power. But this faith is shaken by his experience during the Holocaust.

Initially, Eliezer's faith is a product of his studies in Jewish mysticism, which teach him that God is everywhere in the world, that nothing exists without God, that in fact everything in the physical world is an "emanation," or reflection, of the divine world. In other words, Eliezer has grown up believing that everything on Earth reflects God's holiness and power. His faith is grounded in the idea that God is everywhere, all the time, that his divinity touches every aspect of his daily life. Since God is good, his studies teach him, and God is everywhere in the world, the world must therefore be good.

Eliezer's faith in the goodness of the world is irreparably shaken, however, by the cruelty and evil he witnesses during the Holocaust. He cannot imagine that the concentration camps' unbelievable, disgusting cruelty could possibly reflect divinity. He wonders how a benevolent God could be part of such depravity and how an omnipotent God could permit such cruelty to take place. His faith is equally shaken by the cruelty and selfishness he sees among the prisoners. If all the prisoners were to unite to oppose the cruel oppression of the Nazis, Eliezer believes, then maybe he could understand the Nazi menace as an evil aberration. He would then be able to maintain the belief that humankind is essentially good. But he sees that the Holocaust exposes the selfishness, evil, and cruelty of which *everybody*—not only the Nazis, but also his fellow prisoners, his fellow Jews, even himself—is capable. If the world is so disgusting and cruel, he feels, then God either must be disgusting and cruel or must not exist at all.

Though this realization seems to annihilate his faith, Eliezer manages to retain some of this faith throughout his experiences. At certain moments—during his first night in the camp and during the hanging of the *pipel*—Eliezer does grapple with his faith, but his struggle should not be confused with a complete abandonment of his faith. This struggle doesn't diminish his belief in God; rather, it is essential to the existence of that belief. When Moshe the Beadle is asked why he prays, he replies, "I pray to the God within me that He will give me the strength to ask Him the right questions." In other words, *questioning* is fundamental to the idea of faith in God. The Holocaust forces Eliezer to ask horrible questions about the nature of good and evil and about whether God exists. But the very fact that he asks these questions reflects his commitment to God.

Discussing his own experience, Wiesel once wrote, "My anger rises up within faith and not outside it." Eliezer's struggle reflects such a sentiment. Only in the lowest moments of his faith does he turn his back on God. Indeed, even when Eliezer says that he has given up on God completely, Wiesel's constant use of religious metaphors undercuts what Eliezer says he believes. Eliezer even refers to biblical passages when he denies his faith. When he fears that he might abandon his father, he prays to God, and, after his father's death, he expresses regret that there was no religious memorial. At the end of the book, even though he has been forever changed by his Holocaust experience, Eliezer emerges with his faith intact.

SILENCE
In one of *Night*'s most famous passages, Eliezer states, "Never shall I forget that nocturnal silence which deprived me, for all eternity, of the desire to live." It is the idea of God's silence that he finds most troubling, as this description of an event at Buna reveals: as the Gestapo hangs a young boy, a man asks, "Where is God?" yet the only response is "[t]otal silence throughout the camp." Eliezer and his companions are left to wonder how an all-knowing, all-powerful God can allow such horror and cruelty to occur, especially to such devout worshipers. The existence of this horror, and the lack of a divine response, forever shakes Eliezer's faith in God.

It is worth noting that God's silence during the hanging of the young boy recalls the story of the Akedah—the Binding of Isaac—found in the Hebrew Scriptures (Genesis 22). In the Akedah, God decides to test the faith of Abraham by asking him to sacrifice his only son, Isaac. Abraham does not doubt his God, and he ties Isaac to a sacrificial altar. He raises a knife to kill the boy, but at the last minute God sends an angel to save Isaac. The angel explains that God merely wanted to test Abraham's faith and, of course, would never permit him to shed innocent blood. Unlike the God in *Night*, the God in the Akedah is not silent.

Night can be read as a reversal of the Akedah story: at the moment of a horrible sacrifice, God does *not* intervene to save innocent lives. There is no angel swooping down as masses burn in the crematorium, or as Eliezer's father lies beaten and bloodied. Eliezer and the other prisoners call out for God, and their only response is silence; during his first night at Birkenau, Eliezer says, "The Eternal . . . was silent. What had I to thank Him for?" The lesson Eliezer learns is the opposite of the lesson taught in the Bible. The moral of the Akedah is that God demands sacrifice but is ultimately compassionate. During the Holocaust, however, Eliezer feels that God's silence demonstrates the absence of divine compassion; as a result, he ultimately questions the very existence of God.

There is also a second type of silence operating throughout *Night*: the silence of the victims, and the lack of resistance to the Nazi threat. When his father is beaten at the end of his life, Eliezer remembers, "I did not move. I was afraid," and he feels guilty about his inaction. It is implied throughout the text that silence and passivity are what allowed the Holocaust to continue. Wiesel's writing of *Night* is itself an attempt to break the silence, to tell loudly and boldly of the atrocities of the Holocaust and, in this way, to try to prevent anything so horrible from ever happening again.

INHUMANITY TOWARD OTHER HUMANS

Eliezer's spiritual struggle owes to his shaken faith not only in God but in everything around him. After experiencing such cruelty, Eliezer can no longer make sense of his world. His disillusionment results from his painful experience with Nazi persecution, but also from the cruelty he sees fellow prisoners inflict on each other. Eliezer also becomes aware of the cruelty of which he himself is capable. Everything he experiences in the war shows him how horribly people can treat one another—a revelation that troubles him deeply.

THEMES

The first insensible cruelty Eliezer experiences is that of the Nazis. Yet, when the Nazis first appear, they do not seem monstrous in any way. Eliezer recounts, "[O]ur first impressions of the Germans were most reassuring. . . . Their attitude toward their hosts was distant, but polite." So many aspects of the Holocaust are incomprehensible, but perhaps the most difficult to understand is how human beings could so callously slaughter millions of innocent victims. Wiesel highlights this incomprehensible tragedy by pulling the Nazis into focus first as human beings, and then, as the memoir shifts to the concentration camps, showing the brutal atrocities that they committed.

Furthermore, *Night* demonstrates that cruelty breeds cruelty. Instead of comforting each other in times of difficulty, the prisoners respond to their circumstances by turning against one another. Near the end of the work, a Kapo says to Eliezer, "Here, every man has to fight for himself and not think of anyone else. . . . Here, there are no fathers, no brothers, no friends. Everyone lives and dies for himself alone." It is significant that a Kapo makes this remark to the narrator, because Kapos were themselves prisoners placed in charge of other prisoners. They enjoyed a relatively better (though still horrendous) quality of life in the camp, but they aided the Nazi mission and often behaved cruelly toward prisoners in their charge. At the beginning of the fifth section, Eliezer refers to them as "functionaries of death." The Kapos' position symbolizes the way the Holocaust's cruelty bred cruelty in its victims, turning people against each other, as self-preservation became the highest virtue.

The Importance of Father-Son Bonds

Eliezer is disgusted with the horrific selfishness he sees around him, especially when it involves the rupture of familial bonds. On three occasions, he mentions sons horribly mistreating fathers: in his brief discussion of the *pipel* who abused his father; his terrible conclusion about the motives of Rabbi Eliahou's son; and his narration of the fight for food that he witnesses on the train to Buchenwald, in which a son beats his father to death. All of these moments of cruelty are provoked by the conditions the prisoners are forced to endure. In order to save themselves, these sons sacrifice their fathers.

Traces of the Akedah story (see SILENCE, above) run through the memoir, particularly in the guilt and sadness that Eliezer feels after his father's death. Despite the love and care he has shown his father, Eliezer feels that he has somehow sacrificed his father for his own safety. This sacrifice is the inverse of the Akedah, in which a father (Abraham) is willing to sacrifice his son (Isaac). *Night's* reversal of this example signifies the way the Holocaust has turned Eliezer's entire world upside down.

Eliezer's descriptions of his behavior toward his father seem to invalidate his guilty feelings. He depends on his father for support, and his love for his father allows him to endure. During the long run to Gleiwitz, he says, "My father's presence was the only thing that stopped me [from allowing myself to die]. . . . I had no right to let myself die. What would he do without me? I was his only support." Their relationship demonstrates that Eliezer's love and solidarity are stronger forces of survival than his instinct for self-preservation.

Motifs

Motifs are recurring structures, contrasts, or literary devices that can help to develop and inform the text's major themes.

Tradition

Judaism is more than simply a religion; it is an entire culture that has, for most of its almost 6,000–year existence, been a dispersed culture, a nation without a country, a people without a home. As a result, memory and tradition play a significant role in Jewish life. In the absence of any geographic continuity, Judaism relies on customs, observances, and traditions, passed down from generation to generation, as the markers and bearers of cultural identity. Hitler and the Nazis wanted not only to destroy the Jewish people but also to humiliate them and eradicate all vestiges of Judaism. As Eliezer relates in *Night,* the Germans desecrated Jewish temples, forced Jews to break dietary laws, and deliberately shaved their heads and tattooed them in violation of Jewish Scripture. The Nazi genocide was an attempt to wipe out an entire people, including all sense of national and cultural unity.

Conversation and storytelling have always been important elements of Jewish folk tradition, and Chlomo's storytelling symbolizes Jewish culture as a whole. His story is interrupted by the arrival of the Nazis, just as the Holocaust attempted to interrupt Jewish history as a whole. Throughout the book, Eliezer clings to tradition, even after his faith has apparently been lost, because it serves as an important link to life outside the Holocaust, beyond the terror and oppression he is experiencing. He struggles with the question of fasting on Yom Kippur. He expresses regret when he forgets to say *Kaddish* (a mourner's prayer) for his deceased friend Akiba Drumer, not because he feels that he has forsaken an obligation to God, but because he feels that he has forsaken his commitment to his fellow Jews and fellow prisoners.

RELIGIOUS OBSERVANCE

During the first sections of *Night,* there are frequent mentions of religion and religious observance. Eliezer begins his story mentioning the Talmud and his Jewish studies and prayer rituals. He is upset that the Nazis desecrate the Sabbath and his synagogue. By the end of *Night,* however, mentions of Jewish observance have almost vanished from the text. Most striking, Eliezer does not mention the *Kaddish* by name after his father's death, and says only that "[t]here were no prayers at his grave. No candles were lit in his memory." By specifically avoiding Jewish terminology, Eliezer implies that religious observance has ceased to be a part of his life. Eliezer's feelings about this loss are ambiguous: he has claimed that he has lost all faith in God, yet there is clearly regret and sadness in his tone when he discusses the lack of a religious memorial for his father.

Although Eliezer's explicit mentions of religion vanish, religious metaphor holds *Night*'s entire narrative structure together. As noted above, the Akedah is a foundational metaphor for the work. Throughout the memoir, furthermore, Wiesel indirectly refers to biblical passages (Psalm 150, for example, when Eliezer discusses his loss of faith) and Jewish tradition (the Nazis' selections on Yom Kippur of which prisoners will die—a cruel version of the Jewish belief that God selects who will live and who will die during the Days of Awe). Though Eliezer claims that religion and faith are no longer part of his life, both nevertheless form a tacit foundation for his entire story.

SYMBOLS

Symbols are objects, characters, figures, or colors used to represent abstract ideas or concepts.

FIRE

Fire appears throughout *Night* as a symbol of the Nazis' cruel power. On the way to Auschwitz-Birkenau, Madame Schächter receives a vision of fire that serves as a premonition of the horror to come. Eliezer also sees the Nazis burning babies in a ditch. Most important, fire is the agent of destruction in the crematoria, where many meet their death at the hands of the Nazis.

The role of fire as a Nazi weapon reverses the role fire plays in the Bible and Jewish tradition. In the Bible, fire is associated with God and divine wrath. God appears to Moses as a burning bush, and vengeful angels wield flaming swords. In postbiblical literature, flame also is a force of divine retribution. In Gehenna—the Jewish version of Hell—the wicked are punished by fire. But in *Night*, it is the wicked who wield the power of fire, using it to punish the innocent. Such a reversal demonstrates how the experience of the Holocaust has upset Eliezer's entire concept of the universe, especially his belief in a benevolent, or even just, God.

NIGHT

The Bible begins with God's creation of the earth. When God first begins his creation, the earth is "without form, and void; and darkness [is] upon the face of the deep" (Genesis 1:2, King James Version). God's first act is to create light and dispel this darkness. Darkness and night therefore symbolize a world without God's presence. In *Night*, Wiesel exploits this allusion. Night always occurs when suffering is worst, and its presence reflects Eliezer's belief that he lives in a world without God. The first time Eliezer mentions that "[n]ight fell" is when his father is interrupted while telling stories and informed about the deportation of Jews. Similarly, it is night when Eliezer first arrives at Birkenau/Auschwitz, and it is night—specifically "pitch darkness"—when the prisoners begin their horrible run from Buna.

Summary & Analysis

Foreword

Summary

Noting his trepidation regarding interviews with foreign journalists, François Mauriac recounts his encounter with a journalist from Tel Aviv, later revealed to be *Night*'s author, Elie Wiesel. Once the conversation began, Mauriac's fears were allayed by the intimate nature of the interview. The two talked about the Nazi occupation of France (1940–1944) during World War II. Mauriac notes that his most haunting memories of the Occupation involve events he did not directly witness—his wife told him about seeing trainloads of Jewish children awaiting deportation at Austerlitz station in Paris. Even though he could not imagine the horror that awaited these prisoners, the image of them packed into trains was enough to shatter his illusions about the progress of Western civilization. He refers to the French Revolution (1789) as an unfulfilled promise of progress, a dream that was initially fractured by the outbreak of World War I (Germany declared war on August 2, 1914) and then smashed by the horrors of the Holocaust.

Wiesel then revealed to Mauriac that he was one of the children in those cattle cars, and Mauriac begins discussing the strengths of *Night*. He talks about the power of Wiesel's story: like the memoir of Anne Frank, a German Jew who died in a concentration camp, it is a deeply personal story, bearing painfully intimate witness to the horrors of World War II. He explains that Wiesel has given a human face to the suffering of the Holocaust by telling his own "different, distinct, unique" account of events. As an individual chronicle of life under the Nazis, Mauriac argues, the work merits attention as an incomparable story.

Mauriac adds that Wiesel's narrative possesses an even more engaging, spiritual dimension. Mauriac focuses on the narrator's struggles with God and religion as the most striking aspect of the work. Quoting one of *Night*'s most famous passages (the "Never shall I forget that night" passage that occurs after the narrator's arrival at Auschwitz), Mauriac explains that he was intensely affected by the narrator's loss of faith, and that this crisis of faith is a profoundly troubling legacy of the Holocaust. As a deeply believing Christian, he writes, he wanted to explain to Wiesel that he views suffering as the cornerstone of faith, not as an impediment to trust in God. He wishes he had been able to explain to Wiesel his faith, trust in God's grace, and confidence in eternal mercy. But, Mauriac concludes, the power of Wiesel's story, particularly the depth of his spiritual crisis, overwhelmed him, and, struck speechless, he "embrace[d] him, weeping."

ANALYSIS

François Mauriac (1885–1970) was a French writer, author of novels, poems, essays, journalism, and plays, and winner of the 1952 Nobel Prize in Literature. He was a devout Roman Catholic whose writings often focus on the struggle between good and evil within human nature and the importance of faith. During World War II, Mauriac's vociferous criticism of the Nazis forced him to go into hiding. He later became a staunch supporter of Charles de Gaulle, the French hero who helped liberate his nation from Nazi occupation in 1944.

According to most accounts, it was Mauriac who persuaded Wiesel to write and publish *Night*. Wiesel had imposed a vow of silence upon himself regarding his experiences in the camps, but Mauriac convinced Wiesel of the importance of sharing his story. Along these lines, it is worth noting that some critics—definitely a minority—feel that Wiesel altered his manuscript to conform to Mauriac's emphasis on bearing witness and the crisis of faith. According to these critics, Wiesel's original manuscript, the voluminous Yiddish version of more than 800 pages titled *Un di Velt Hot Geshvign* (*And the World Remained Silent*), is much fiercer in tone than *Night*. These same critics argue that Mauriac's influence caused Wiesel to remove the manuscript's vitriol and its demands for retribution in favor of a more somber, reflective, and harrowing—and consequently more palatable and sympathetic—tone.

These criticisms aside, Mauriac's foreword insightfully points to the true strengths of Wiesel's work. *Night* is a terrifyingly personal account of horrific events. As Mauriac points out, the Nazi atrocities were so unimaginable and inconceivable that, merely by bearing witness, Wiesel is performing an invaluable service to humanity. As Mauriac illustrates with the anecdote about his wife, we cannot always see firsthand the horrible suffering of the world, but it is imperative that we are told about it and recognize its horror. As he notes, "It is not always the events we have been directly involved in that affect us the most." By bearing witness, by sharing his incredibly painful and personal story, Wiesel enables us to better understand a horrific historical moment that is impossible to imagine in the abstract.

Mauriac also focuses on the power of the narrator's crisis of faith and the loss of his faith in God. This loss of faith, however, is not quite as complete as Mauriac suggests. Wiesel's struggles with God are much more complex than a simple journey from complete faith to a belief that God no longer exists. Nevertheless, it is interesting that Mauriac frames Wiesel's loss of faith as, paradoxically, an affirmation of Christian conceptions of God. Mauriac explains that the idea of suffering, of pain and persecution, is fundamental to his conceptions of Jesus Christ and his religious beliefs. Christians, he argues, accept that the world is full of suffering, and this recognition of suffering increases belief in grace. Because the world is so corrupt, he implies, a Christian is able to believe more fully in the purity of divine law and mercy. But, in the end, Mauriac acknowledges that the basic human emotions he feels when presented with Wiesel's story overwhelm such a theoretical argument. *Night* is remarkable for its intellectual, spiritual, and theological depth, but its greatest power, it is clear, lies in its emotional candor.

SECTION ONE

SUMMARY

NOTE: *This SparkNote is divided into nine sections, following the organization of* Night. *Though Wiesel did not number his sections, this SparkNote has added numbers for ease of reference.*

In 1941, Eliezer, the narrator, is a twelve-year-old boy living in the Transylvanian town of Sighet (then recently annexed to Hungary, now part of Romania). He is the only son in an Orthodox Jewish family that strictly adheres to Jewish tradition and law. His parents are shopkeepers, and his father is highly respected within Sighet's Jewish community. Eliezer has two older sisters, Hilda and Béa, and a younger sister named Tzipora.

Eliezer studies the Talmud, the Jewish oral law. He also studies the Jewish mystical texts of the Cabbala (often spelled Kabbalah), a somewhat unusual occupation for a teenager, and one that goes against his father's wishes. Eliezer finds a sensitive and challenging teacher in Moshe the Beadle, a local pauper. Soon, however, the Hungarians expel all foreign Jews, including Moshe. Despite their momentary anger, the Jews of Sighet soon forget about this anti-Semitic act. After several months, having escaped his captors, Moshe returns and tells how the deportation trains were handed over to the Gestapo (German secret police) at the Polish border. There, he explains, the Jews were forced to dig mass graves for themselves and were killed by the Gestapo. The town takes him for a lunatic and refuses to believe his story.

In the spring of 1944, the Hungarian government falls into the hands of the Fascists, and the next day the German armies occupy Hungary. Despite the Jews' belief that Nazi anti-Semitism would be limited to the capital city, Budapest, the Germans soon move into Sighet. A series of increasingly oppressive measures are forced on the Jews—the community leaders are arrested, Jewish valuables are confiscated, and all Jews are forced to wear yellow stars. Eventually, the Jews are confined to small ghettos, crowded together into narrow streets behind barbed-wire fences.

The Nazis then begin to deport the Jews in increments, and Eliezer's family is among the last to leave Sighet. They watch as other Jews are crowded into the streets in the hot sun, carrying only what fits in packs on their backs. Eliezer's family is first herded into another, smaller ghetto. Their former servant, a gentile named Martha, visits them and offers to hide them in her village. Tragically, they decline the offer. A few days later, the Nazis and their henchmen, the Hungarian police, herd the last Jews remaining in Sighet onto cattle cars bound for Auschwitz.

ANALYSIS

One of the enduring questions that has tormented the Jews of Europe who survived the Holocaust is whether or not they might have been able to escape the Holocaust had they acted more wisely. A shrouded doom hangs behind every word in this first section of *Night,* in which Wiesel laments the typical human inability to acknowledge the depth of the cruelty of which humans are capable. The Jews of Sighet are unable or unwilling to believe in the horrors of Hitler's death camps, even though there are many instances in which they have glimpses of what awaits them. Eliezer relates that many Jews do not believe that Hitler really intends to annihilate them, even though he can trace the steps by which the Nazis made life in Hungary increasingly unbearable for the Jews. Furthermore, he painfully details the cruelty with which the Jews are treated during their deportation. He even asks his father to move the family to Palestine and escape whatever is to come, but his father is unwilling to leave Sighet behind. We, as readers whom history has made less naïve than the Jews of Sighet, sense what is to come, how annihilation draws inexorably closer to the Jews, and watch helplessly as the Jews fail to see, or refuse to acknowledge, their fate.

The story of Moshe the Beadle, with which *Night* opens, is perhaps the most painful example of the Jews' refusal to believe the depth of Nazi evil. It is also a cautionary tale about the danger of refusing to heed firsthand testimony, a tale that explains the urgency behind Wiesel's own account. Moshe, who escapes from a Nazi massacre and returns to Sighet to warn the villagers of the truth about the deportations, is treated as a madman. What is crucial for Wiesel is that his own testimony, as a survivor of the Holocaust, not be ignored. Moshe's example in this section is a reminder that the cost of ignoring witnesses to evil is a recurrence of that evil.

If one of Wiesel's goals is to prevent the Holocaust from recurring by bearing witness to it, another is the preservation of the memory of the victims. Eliezer's relationship with his father is a continuous theme in Wiesel's memoir. He documents their mutually supportive relationship, Eliezer's growing feeling that his father is a burden to him, and his guilt about that feeling.

On a larger scale, Wiesel also hopes to preserve the memory of the Jewish tradition through his portrayal of his father. When news of the deportations comes to Sighet, Eliezer's father, a respected community leader, is among the first notified. He is in the middle of telling a story when he is forced to leave. Wiesel notes, "The good story he had been in the middle of telling us was to remain unfinished." In a metaphorical sense, this "good story" symbolizes the entirety of European Jewish tradition, transmitted to Eliezer—and to Wiesel himself—through the father figure. *Night* laments the loss of this tradition, of the story that remains unfinished. In writing this memoir and his other works, Wiesel is attempting to complete his father's story, honor the memory of the Holocaust victims, and commemorate the traditions they left behind.

The first section of *Night* also establishes the groundwork for Eliezer's later struggle with his faith. At the start of the story, he is a devout Jew from a devout community. He studies Jewish tradition faithfully and believes faithfully in God. As the Jews are deported, they continue to express their trust that God will save them from the Nazis: "Oh God, Lord of the Universe, take pity upon us...." Eliezer's experience in the concentration camps, however, eventually leads to his loss of faith, because he decides that he cannot believe in a God who would allow such suffering.

Later in the memoir, Eliezer suggests that, for him, one of the most horrible of the Nazis' deeds was their metaphorical murder of God. Since the Holocaust, Judaism has been forced to confront the long-existent problem of theodicy—how God can exist and permit such evil. *Night* chronicles Eliezer's loss of innocence, his confrontation with evil, and his questioning of God's existence.

SECTION TWO

SUMMARY

Packed into cattle cars, the Jews are tormented by nearly unbearable conditions. There is almost no air to breathe, the heat is intense, there is no room to sit, and everyone is hungry and thirsty. In their fear, the Jews begin to lose their sense of public decorum. Some men and women begin to flirt openly on the train as though they were alone, while others pretend not to notice. After days of travel in these inhuman conditions, the train arrives at the Czechoslovakian border, and the Jews realize that they are not simply being relocated. A German officer takes official charge of the train, threatening to shoot any Jew who refuses to yield his or her valuables and to exterminate everybody in the car if anybody escapes. The doors to the car are nailed shut, further preventing escape.

Madame Schächter, a middle-aged woman who is on the train with her ten-year- old son, soon cracks under the oppressive treatment to which the Jews are subjected. On the third night, she begins to scream that she sees a fire in the darkness outside the car. Although no fire is visible, she terrifies the Jews in the car, who are reminded that they do not know what awaits them. But, as with Moshe the Beadle earlier in the memoir, they console themselves in the belief that Madame Schächter is crazy. Finally, she is tied up and gagged so that she cannot scream. Her child, sitting next to her, watches and cries. When Madame Schächter breaks out of her bonds and continues to scream about the furnace that awaits them, she is beaten into silence by some of the boys on the train, with the encouragement of the others. The next night, Madame Schächter begins her screaming again.

The prisoners on the train find out, when the train eventually stops, that they have reached Auschwitz station. This name means nothing to them, and they bribe some locals to get news. They are told that they have arrived at a labor camp where they will be treated well and kept together as families. This news comes as a relief, and the prisoners let themselves believe, again, that all will be well. With nightfall, however, Madame Schächter again wakes everyone with her screams, and again she is beaten into silence. The train moves slowly and at midnight passes into an area enclosed by barbed wire. Through the windows, everybody sees the chimneys of vast furnaces. There is a terrible, but undefined, odor in the air—what they soon discover is the odor of burning human flesh. This concentration camp is Birkenau, the processing center for arrivals at Auschwitz.

ANALYSIS

One of Wiesel's concerns in *Night* is the way that exposure to inhuman cruelty can deprive even victims of their sense of morality and humanity. By treating the Jews as less than human, the Nazis cause the Jews to *act* as if they were less than human—cruelty breeds cruelty, Wiesel demonstrates. In the ghetto, Eliezer recounts, the Jews maintained their social cohesion, their sense of common purpose and common morality. Once robbed of their homes and treated like animals, however, they begin to *act* like animals. The first hint of this dehumanized behavior on the part of the Jewish prisoners comes when some of the deportees, in the constraints of the cattle car, lose their modesty and sense of sexual inhibition. As the section progresses, the Jews become more and more depraved, overcome by their terror. Some of them begin to beat Madame Schächter in order to quiet her, and others vocally support those who are doing the beating. Wiesel suggests that one of the great psychological and moral tragedies of the Holocaust is not just the death of faith in God but also the death of faith in humankind. Not only does God fail to act justly and save the Jews from the cruel Nazis; the Nazis drive the Jews into cruelty, so that the Jews themselves fail to act justly.

The Jewish prisoners' continual denial of what is happening around them reflects one of the major barriers in writing about the Holocaust. Until the Jews experience the horrors of Auschwitz, they cannot believe that such horrors exist. Even after having heard Moshe's firsthand report, when the Jews arrive at Auschwitz, they still believe that it is merely a work camp. One can imagine, then, how difficult it is to convince others of the atrocities committed by the Nazis. Wiesel reminds us that the Holocaust is almost too awful a story to convey, yet he insists that it is a story that must be told, because it is crucial that those who hear the story believe, and act on their beliefs, before it is too late.

The figure of Madame Schächter, who in her lunacy foresees the furnaces of Auschwitz, raises an important question about the boundaries between sanity and insanity in the context of the evils of the Holocaust. Madame Schächter, who is supposedly crazy, sees clearly into the future, whereas the other Jews, who are supposedly sane, fail to foresee their fate. Throughout Wiesel's memoir, sanity and insanity become confused in the face of atrocity. One would think it insane to imagine the extermination of six million Jews, yet it occurred, efficiently and methodically. In the world of Auschwitz, then, normal standards of lunacy and sanity become confused, just as one's sense of morality is turned upside down.

SECTION THREE

Never shall I forget these things, even if I am
condemned to live as long as God Himself. Never.
(See QUOTATIONS, p. 45)

SUMMARY

At Birkenau, the first of many "selections" occurs, during which individuals presumed weaker or less useful are weeded out to be killed. Eliezer and his father remain together, separated from Eliezer's mother and younger sister, whom he never sees again. Eliezer and his father meet a prisoner, who counsels them to lie about their ages. Eliezer, not yet fifteen, is to say that he is eighteen, while his father, who is fifty, is to say that he is forty. Another prisoner accosts the new arrivals, angrily asking them why they peacefully let the Nazis bring them to Auschwitz. He explains to them, finally, why they have been brought to Auschwitz: to be killed and burned. Hearing this, some among the younger Jews begin to consider rebelling, but the older Jews advise them to rely not on rebellion but on faith, and they proceed docilely to the selection. In a central square, Dr. Mengele stands, determining whether new arrivals are fit to work or whether they are to be killed immediately. Taking the prisoner's advice, Eliezer lies about his age, telling Mengele he is eighteen. He also says that he is a farmer rather than a student, and is motioned to Mengele's left, along with his father.

Despite Eliezer's joy at remaining with his father, uncertainty remains. Nobody knows whether left means the crematorium or the prison. As the prisoners move through Birkenau, they are horrified to see a huge pit where babies are being burned, and another for adults. Eliezer cannot believe his eyes, and tells his father that what they see is impossible, that "humanity would never tolerate" such an atrocity. His father, breaking down into tears, replies that humanity is nonexistent in the world of the crematoria. Everybody in the column of prisoners weeps, and somebody begins to recite the Jewish prayer for the dead, the *Kaddish*. Eliezer's father also recites the prayer. Eliezer, however, is skeptical. He cannot understand what he has to thank God for. When Eliezer and his father are two steps from the edge of the pit, their rank is diverted and directed to a barracks. Eliezer interrupts his narration with a moving reflection on the impact of that night on his life, a night that forever burned Nazi atrocity into his memory.

In the barracks, the Jews are stripped and shaved, disinfected with gasoline, showered, and clothed in prison uniforms. They are lectured by a Nazi officer and told that they have two options: hard work or the crematorium. When Eliezer's father asks for the bathroom, he is beaten by the Kapo (a head prisoner, in charge of the other inmates). Eliezer is appalled at his own failure to defend his father. Soon they make the short march from Birkenau to Auschwitz, where they are quartered for three weeks, and where their prison numbers are tattooed on their arms. Eliezer and his father meet a distant relative from Antwerp, a man named Stein, who inquires after news of his family. Eliezer's father lies and tells him that he has heard about Stein's family, and that they are alive and well. When a transport from Antwerp arrives, however, the man learns the truth, and he never visits Eliezer again.

Despite all that they have seen, the prisoners continue to express their faith in God and trust in divine redemption. Finally, they are escorted on a four-hour walk from Auschwitz to Buna, the work camp in which they will be interned for months.

ANALYSIS

As a work of literature, *Night* stands on the borderline between fiction and memoir. Wiesel breaks conventions of traditional fiction writing in order to tell the truth about historical events. For example, at the beginning of this section, Eliezer is separated from his mother and sister, whom he never sees again. Presumably, they both die in the Holocaust, just as Wiesel's own mother and younger sister did. Remarkably, Eliezer's mother and sister are never mentioned again in *Night*. It is as if they simply disappear from Eliezer's mind and memory. Such a disappearance would probably not happen in a novel, since novels generally are careful about keeping track of all of their characters. Thus, the disappearance of these two characters is a powerful reminder of the necessarily fragmentary nature of memory and memoir.

Wiesel's chilling first-person narration results in a powerful immediacy of emotion. He shows us only what Eliezer sees and thinks at a given moment—his limited perspective and lack of knowledge make the story all the more terrifying. It is as if the reader is with Eliezer, caught up in the tension and horror of his experience. This kind of narration does not permit more leisurely reflection about events that are not occurring immediately, or not occurring in the vicinity of the narrator. *Night* is not meant to offer an extended autobiography of Wiesel. While his two works of autobiography, *All Rivers Run to the Sea* and *And the Sea Is Never Full*, do in fact dwell on his sorrow at losing his mother and sister, *Night* is not intended to be comprehensive. Instead, it is intended as a brief, harrowing portrait of Wiesel's life during the Holocaust.

Eliezer's loss of faith in God begins at Auschwitz. When he first sees the furnace pits in which the Nazis are burning babies, he experiences the beginnings of doubt: "Why should I bless His name?" Eliezer asks, "What had I to thank Him for?" Though not complete at that moment, Eliezer's loss of faith contrasts with the continued faith of such devout prisoners as Akiba Drumer, whose faith in divine redemption raises the prisoners' spirits.

We also see, as Eliezer begins to doubt his own humanity, the beginning of his loss of faith in man. When the Kapo beats his father, Eliezer wonders at the transformation that he himself has undergone. Only the day before, he tells himself, he would have attacked the Kapo; now, however, he remains guiltily silent. Fear of silence figures prominently in this memoir, as it is silence in the face of evil, Wiesel believes, that allows evil to survive.

This section contains perhaps the most famous, and the most moving, paragraphs in all of *Night*. Only rarely does Eliezer interrupt his continuous narrative stream to reminisce about the ways that the Holocaust continued to affect his life after it ended. Here, however, Eliezer looks back on his first night in Birkenau and describes not only what he felt at the time but also the lasting impact of that night:

> Never shall I forget that night . . . which has turned my life into one long night . . . .
> Never shall I forget those flames which consumed my faith forever.
> Never shall I forget that nocturnal silence which deprived me, for all eternity, of the desire to live. Never shall I forget those moments which murdered my God. . . . Never shall I forget these things, even if I am condemned to live as long as God Himself. Never.

The repetition of the phrase "Never shall I forget" illustrates how Eliezer's experiences are forever burned into his mind; like the actual experiences, the memories of them are inescapable. The phrase seems also like a personal mantra for Wiesel, who understands the crucial necessity of remembering the horrible events of the Holocaust and bringing them to light so that nothing like them can ever happen again.

SECTION FOUR

SUMMARY

> *"Where is God now?"*
> *And I heard a voice within me answer him:*
> *"Where is He? Here He is—He is hanging here on*
> *this gallows. . . ."*   (See QUOTATIONS, p. 47)

After the required quarantine and medical inspection—including a dental search for gold crowns—Eliezer is chosen by a Kapo to serve in a unit of prisoners whose job entails counting electrical fittings in a civilian warehouse. His father, it turns out, serves in the same unit. Eliezer and his father are to be housed in the musicians' block, which is headed by a kindly German Jew. In this block of prisoners, Eliezer meets Juliek, a Jewish violinist, and the brothers Yosi and Tibi. With the brothers, who are Zionists (they favor the creation of a Jewish homeland in Palestine, the holy land), Eliezer plans to move to Palestine after the war is over. Akiba Drumer, his faith still strong, predicts that deliverance from the camps is imminent.

Not long after Eliezer and his father arrive in Buna, Eliezer is summoned to the dentist to have his gold crown pulled. He manages to plead illness and postpone having the crown removed. Soon after, the dentist is condemned to hanging for illegally trading in gold teeth. Eliezer does not pity the dentist, because he has become too busy keeping his body intact and finding food to eat to spare any pity. Idek, the Kapo in charge of Eliezer's work crew, is prone to fits of violent madness. One day, unprovoked, he savagely beats Eliezer, after which a French girl who works next to Eliezer in the warehouse offers some small kindness and comfort.

The narrator then skips forward several years to recount how, after the Holocaust, he runs into the same girl—now a woman—on the Métro in Paris. He explains that he recognized her, and she told him her story: she was a Jew passing as an Aryan on forged papers; she worked in the warehouse as a laborer but was not a concentration camp prisoner.

The narration then returns to Eliezer's time at Buna. Eliezer's father falls victim to one of Idek's rages. Painfully honest, Eliezer reveals how much the concentration camp has changed him. He is concerned, at that moment, only with his own survival. Rather than feel angry at Idek, Eliezer becomes angry at his father for his inability to dodge Idek's fury.

When Franek, the prison foreman, notices Eliezer's gold crown, he demands it. Franek's desire for the gold makes him vicious and cruel. On his father's advice, Eliezer refuses to yield the tooth. As punishment, Franek mocks and beats Eliezer's father until Eliezer eventually gives up. Soon after this incident, both Idek and Franek, along with the other Polish prisoners, are transferred to another camp. Before this happens, however, Eliezer accidentally witnesses Idek having sex in the barracks. In punishment, Idek publicly whips Eliezer until he loses consciousness.

During an Allied air raid on Buna, during which every prisoner is supposed to be confined to his or her block, two cauldrons of soup are left unattended. Eliezer and many other prisoners watch as a man risks his life to crawl to the soup. The man reaches the soup, and after a moment of hesitation lifts himself up to eat. As he stands over the soup, he is shot and falls lifeless to the ground. A week later, the Nazis erect a gallows in the central square and publicly hang another man who had attempted to steal something during the air raid. Eliezer tells the tale of another hanging, that of two prisoners suspected of being involved with the resistance and of a young boy who was the servant of a resistance member. Although the prisoners are all so jaded by suffering that they never cry, they all break into tears as they watch the child strangle on the end of the noose. One man wonders how God could be present in a world with such cruelty. Eliezer, mourning, thinks that, as far as he is concerned, God has been murdered on the gallows together with the child.

Analysis

The harrowing scene of the child's murder with which this section concludes symbolically enacts the murder of God. Eliezer comes to believe that a just God must not exist in a world where an innocent child can be hanged on the gallows. "Where is He?" Eliezer asks rhetorically, and then answers, "He is hanging here on this gallows." Upon witnessing the hanging of the child, Eliezer reaches the low point of his faith.

The death of the innocent child represents the death of Eliezer's own innocence. In the camp, he has become someone different from the child he was at the beginning of the Holocaust. He has lost his faith, and he is beginning to lose his sense of morals and values as well. In a world in which survival is nearly impossible, survival has become Eliezer's dominant goal. He admits that he lives only to feed himself. When his father is beaten, Eliezer feels no pity. Instead, he becomes angry at his father for failing to learn, as Eliezer is learning, how to survive without attracting the anger of the overseers.

Eliezer's relationship with his father is all-important to both of them, because it provides both with support. Though it is crucial to Eliezer to remain with his father at all costs, even the link between parent and child grows tenuous under the stress of the Nazi oppression. When, in this section, Eliezer relates with horror a story about witnessing a thirteen-year-old child who beats his father for making his bed improperly, he seems to feel that the event serves as an implicit cautionary tale. It is Eliezer's great fear that he too will lose his sense of kindness and filial responsibility, that he may turn against his father to facilitate his own survival.

Eliezer's story of his encounter with the French girl who comforts him after he is beaten by Idek the Kapo is unusual because it is one of the few places in the memoir where he jumps into the future to explain what happened after the liberation of the concentration camps. This chance meeting on the métro is the kind of coincidental twist that a novelist might invent but that rarely occurs in nonfiction because it rarely occurs in real life. Several such coincidences do happen in *Night,* however—for example, Eliezer meets Juliek again later in the memoir—but none of them lessens the truthful impact of the story.

In Wiesel's mind, the fact of surviving the Holocaust is in itself a staggeringly unlikely coincidence, a stroke of sheer luck. The overwhelming majority of concentration camp prisoners did not survive. If one can survive in the face of such great odds, then any coincidence becomes believable. Wiesel wants to make the point that his own survival is a result of luck and coincidence. To attribute his survival to his own merit would be inaccurate, as well as disrespectful of the memories of those millions who did not survive.

SECTION FIVE

SUMMARY

At the end of the summer of 1944, the Jewish High Holidays arrive: Rosh Hashanah, the celebration of the new year, and Yom Kippur, the Day of Atonement. Despite their imprisonment and affliction, the Jews of Buna come together to celebrate Rosh Hashanah, praying together and praising God's name. On this solemn Jewish holiday, Eliezer's religious rebellion intensifies, and he cannot find a reason to bless God in the midst of so much suffering. Eliezer mocks the idea that the Jews are God's chosen people, deciding that they have only been chosen to be massacred. He comes to believe that man is stronger than God, more resilient and more forgiving. His denial of faith leaves him alone, or so he believes, among the 10,000 Jewish celebrants in Buna. Leaving the service, however, Eliezer finds his father, and there is a moment of communion and understanding between them. Searching his father's face, Eliezer finds only despair. Eliezer decides to eat on Yom Kippur, the day on which Jews traditionally fast in order to atone for their sins.

Soon after the Jewish New Year, another selection is announced. Eliezer has been separated from his father to work in the building unit. He worries that his father will not pass the selection, and after several days it turns out that Eliezer's father is indeed one of those deemed too weak to work: he will be executed. He brings Eliezer his knife and spoon, his son's only inheritance. Eliezer is then forced to leave, never to see his father again.

When Eliezer returns from work, it seems to him that there has been a miracle. A second selection occurred among the condemned, and Eliezer's father survived. Akiba Drumer, however, is not so lucky. Having lost his faith, he loses his will to live and does not survive the selection. Others are also beginning to lose their faith. Eliezer tells of a devout rabbi who confesses that he can no longer believe in God after what he has seen in the concentration camps.

With the arrival of winter, the prisoners begin to suffer in the cold. Eliezer's foot swells up, and he undergoes an operation. While he is in the hospital recovering, the rumor of the approaching Russian army gives him new hope. But the Germans decide to evacuate the camp before the Russians can arrive. Thinking that the Jews in the infirmary will be put to death prior to the evacuation, Eliezer and his father choose to be evacuated with the others. After the war, Eliezer learns that they made the wrong decision—those who remained in the infirmary were freed by the Russians a few days later. With his injured foot bleeding into the snow, Eliezer joins the rest of the prisoners. At nightfall, in the middle of a snowstorm, they begin their evacuation of Buna.

ANALYSIS

In Jewish tradition, the High Holidays are the time of divine judgment. According to the prayer book, Jews pass before God on Rosh Hashanah like sheep before the shepherd, and God determines who will live and who will die in the coming year. In the concentration camps, Eliezer hints, a horrible reversal has taken place. Soon after Rosh Hashanah, the SS (Nazi police) performs a selection on the prisoners at Buna. All the prisoners pass before Dr. Mengele, the notoriously cruel Nazi doctor, and he determines who is condemned to death and who can go on living. The parallel is clear and so is the message: the Nazis have placed themselves in God's role. Eliezer has decided that the Nazis' actions mean that God is not present in the concentration camps, and thus praying to him is foolish.

The Nazis' usurpation of God's role is further emphasized when an inmate tells Eliezer, "I've got more faith in Hitler than in anyone else. He's the only one who's kept his promises . . . to the Jewish people." Akiba Drumer's death makes it painfully clear that humankind requires faith and hope to live. After losing his faith, Drumer resigns himself to death. Eliezer promises to say the *Kaddish,* the prayer for the dead, on Drumer's behalf, but he forgets his promise. Eliezer's loss of faith comes to mean betrayal not just of God but also of his fellow human beings. Wiesel seems to affirm that life without faith or hope of some kind is empty. Yet, even in rejecting God, Eliezer and his fellow Jews cannot erase God from their consciousness. Though he has supposedly lost his faith in God, Akiba Drumer requests that Eliezer say the *Kaddish* on his behalf; clearly religion still holds some power over him. Similarly, in the third section, Eliezer, having rejected his faith in God forever, still refers to God's existence when making his oath never to forget the Holocaust "even if I am condemned to live as long as God Himself." In the first volume of his autobiography, *All Rivers Run to the Sea,* Wiesel speaks at far greater length about his religious feelings after the Holocaust. "My anger rises up within faith and not outside it," he writes. "I had seen too much suffering to break with the past and reject the heritage of those who had suffered." Wiesel, in his personal life, kept his faith in God throughout the Holocaust. His narrator, Eliezer, seems unable to reject the Jewish tradition and the Jewish God completely, even though he declares his loss of faith.

As *Night* is a record of Wiesel's feelings during the Holocaust, it is often seen as a work that offers no hope at all. Though it ends with Eliezer a shattered young man, faithless and without hope for himself or for humanity, it is Wiesel's belief that there are reasons to believe in both God and humankind's capacity for goodness, even after the Holocaust. One might argue that the very existence of *Night* demonstrates Eliezer's continued belief in the importance of human life in general and his own life in particular. It would seem incongruous to write a memoir if, as Eliezer swears in Section Three, he has forever lost his will to live. The mere fact of writing *Night* seems to conflict with Eliezer's hopelessness.

SECTIONS SIX–SEVEN

At last, the morning star appeared in the gray sky. A
trail of indeterminate light showed on the horizon.
We were exhausted. We were without strength,
without illusions.   (See QUOTATIONS, p. 48)

SUMMARY

In the blizzard and the darkness, the prisoners from Buna are evacuated. Anybody who stops running is shot by the SS. Zalman, a boy running alongside Eliezer, decides he can run no further. He stops and is trampled to death. Malnourished, exhausted, and weakened by his injured foot, Eliezer forces himself to run along with the other prisoners only for the sake of his father, who is running near him. After running all night and covering more than forty-two miles, the prisoners find themselves in a deserted village.

Father and son keep each other awake—falling asleep in the cold would be deadly—and support each other, surviving only through mutual vigilance. Rabbi Eliahou, a kindly and beloved old man, finds his way into the shed where Eliezer and his father are collapsed. The rabbi is looking for his son: throughout their ordeal in the concentration camps, father and son have protected and supported each other. Eliezer falsely tells Rabbi Eliahou he has not seen the son, yet, during the run, Eliezer saw the son abandon his father, running ahead when it seemed Rabbi Eliahou would not survive. Eliezer prays that he will never do what Rabbi Eliahou's son did.

At last, the exhausted prisoners arrive at the Gleiwitz camp, crushing each other in the rush to enter the barracks. In the press of men, Eliezer and his father are thrown to the ground. Fighting for air, Eliezer discovers that he is lying on top of Juliek, the musician who befriended him in Buna. Eliezer soon finds that he himself is in danger of being crushed to death by the man lying on top of him. He finally gains some breathing room, and, calling out, discovers that his father is near. Among the dying men, the sound of Juliek's violin pierces the silence. Eliezer falls asleep to this music, and when he wakes he finds Juliek dead, his violin smashed. After three days without bread and water, there is another selection. When Eliezer's father is sent to stand among those condemned to die, Eliezer runs after him. In the confusion that follows, both Eliezer and his father are able to sneak back over to the other side. The prisoners are taken to a field, where a train of roofless cattle cars comes to pick them up.

The prisoners are herded into the cattle cars and ordered to throw out the bodies of the dead men. Eliezer's father, unconscious, is almost mistaken for dead and thrown from the car, but Eliezer succeeds in waking him. The train travels for ten days and nights, and the Jews go unfed, living on snow. As they pass through German towns, some of the locals throw bread into the car in order to enjoy watching the Jews kill each other for the food. Eliezer then flashes forward to an experience he has after the Holocaust, when he sees a rich Parisian tourist in Aden (a city in Yemen) throwing coins to native boys. Two of the desperately poor boys try to kill each other over one of the coins, but when Eliezer asks the Parisian woman to stop, she replies, "I like to give charity."

Eliezer then returns to his narration of the German townspeople throwing bread on the train. An old man manages to grab a piece, but Eliezer watches as he is attacked and beaten to death by his own son, who in turn is beaten to death by other men. One night, someone tries to strangle Eliezer in his sleep. Eliezer's father calls Meir Katz, a strong friend of theirs, who rescues Eliezer, but Meir Katz himself is losing hope. When the train arrives at Buchenwald, only twelve out of the 100 men who were in Eliezer's train car are still alive. Meir Katz is among the dead.

> *My God, Lord of the Universe, give me strength never to do what Rabbi Eliahou's son has done.*
> (See QUOTATIONS, p. 49)

ANALYSIS

In these sections, we are told two particularly striking stories about sons and fathers. Rabbi Eliahou's son abandons him during the death march from Buna, and a nameless son, in the cattle cars from Gleiwitz to Buchenwald, beats his father to death for a crust of bread. In addition to illustrating the depth of the brutality to which people are capable of sinking when they are mistreated for too long, these incidents reflect on another of the memoir's central themes. They examine the way that the Holocaust tests father-son bonds.

The test of the father-son relationship recalls the biblical story of the Binding of Isaac, known in Hebrew as the Akedah. Critics have suggested that *Night* is a reversal of the Akedah story. The story, related in Genesis, tells of God's commandment to Abraham to sacrifice his son Isaac as an offering. Utterly faithful, Abraham complies with God's wish. Just as Abraham is about to sacrifice Isaac, God intervenes and saves Isaac, rewarding Abraham for his faithfulness. *Night* reverses the Akedah story—the father is sacrificed so that his son might live. But in *Night*, God fails to appear to save the sacrificial victim at the last moment. In the world of the Holocaust, Wiesel argues, God is powerless, or silent.

Eliezer never sinks to the level of beating his father, or outwardly mistreating him, but his resentment toward his father grows, even as it is suggested—for instance, when Eliezer's father prevents Eliezer from killing himself by falling asleep in the snow—that the father is sacrificing himself for his son, not vice versa. Whether or not this resentment comes to dominate Eliezer's relationship with his father (indeed, a strong argument can be made for Eliezer's altruism), it seems clear that Eliezer himself feels great guilt at his father's death. As has been suggested, this guilt perhaps drives Eliezer to feel that he must record the events of the Holocaust, honor his father's memory, and repay his sacrifice.

Eliezer's discussion of the German townspeople who cruelly throw bread to the starving Jews to watch them fight to the death over the crusts of bread is another instance of Eliezer flashing forward into the future to illustrate how the Holocaust has forever altered his understanding of humankind. His digression is rare because it relates an event in which he was not a direct participant; he was a casual witness, and the event was tangential to his life. The parallel between the Parisian woman's "charity" and the actions of the German townspeople is clear, however, and Wiesel tells the story to show that behavior that is casually cruel is not limited to the Holocaust—humanity has an unimaginably wicked streak in it.

SECTIONS EIGHT–NINE

> *From the depths of the mirror, a corpse gazed back at me. The look in his eyes, as they stared into mine, has never left me.* (See QUOTATIONS, p. 50)

SUMMARY

The journey to Buchenwald has fatally weakened Eliezer's father. On arrival, he sits in the snow and refuses to move. He seems at last to have given in to death. Eliezer tries to convince him to move, but he will not or cannot, asking only to be allowed to rest. When an air raid alert drives everyone into the barracks, Eliezer leaves his father

SUMMARY & ANALYSIS

and falls deeply asleep. In the morning, he begins to search for his father, but halfheartedly. Part of him thinks that he will be better off if he abandons his father and conserves his strength. Almost accidentally, however, he finds his father, who is very sick and unable to move. Eliezer brings him soup and coffee. Again, however, Eliezer feels deep guilt, because part of him would rather keep the food for himself, to increase his own chance of survival.

Confined to his bed, Eliezer's father continues to approach death. He is afflicted with dysentery, which makes him terribly thirsty, but it is extremely dangerous to give water to a man with dysentery. Eliezer tries to find medical help for his father, to no avail. The doctors will not treat the old man. The prisoners whose beds surround Eliezer's father's bed steal his food and beat him. Eliezer, unable to resist his father's cries for help, gives him water. After a week, Eliezer is approached by the head of the block, who tells him what he already knows—that Eliezer's father is dying, and that Eliezer should concentrate his energy on his own survival. The next time the ss patrol the barracks, Eliezer's father again cries for water, and the ss officer, screaming at Eliezer's father to shut up, beats him in the head with his truncheon. The next morning, January 29, 1945, Eliezer wakes up to find that his father has been taken to the crematory. To his deep shame, he does not cry. Instead, he feels relief.

Eliezer remains in Buchenwald, thinking neither of liberation nor of his family, but only of food. On April 5, with the American army approaching, the Nazis decide to annihilate all the Jews left in the camp. Daily, thousands of Jews are murdered. On April 10, with about 20,000 people remaining in the camp, the Nazis decide to evacuate—and kill—everyone left in the camp. As the evacuation begins, however, an air-raid siren sounds, sending everybody indoors. When it seems that all has returned to normal and that the evacuation will proceed as planned, the resistance movement strikes, driving the ss from the camp. Hours later, on April 11, the American army arrives at Buchenwald. Now free, the prisoners think only of feeding themselves. Eliezer is struck with food poisoning and spends weeks in the hospital, deathly ill. When he finally raises himself and looks in the mirror—he has not seen himself in a mirror since leaving Sighet—he is shocked: "From the depths of the mirror," Wiesel writes, "a corpse gazed back at me."

ANALYSIS

Although we know that Elie Wiesel, *Night*'s author, recovered his faith in man and God and went on to lead a productive life after the Holocaust, none of this post-Holocaust biographical information is present in *Night*. Because the scope of *Night* does not extend beyond Eliezer's liberation, some readers argue that the memoir offers no hope whatsoever. Eliezer has been witness to the ultimate evil; he has lost his faith in God, and in the souls of men. *Night*'s final line, in which Eliezer looks at himself in the mirror and sees a "corpse," suggests that Eliezer's survival is a stroke of luck, a strange coincidence, no cause for rejoicing. It seems from his closing vision that Eliezer believes that without hope and faith, after having seen the unimaginable, he might as well be dead.

After stating that he sees a "corpse" looking back at him, Eliezer adds, "The look in his eyes, as they stared into mine, has never left me." While it is true that Eliezer, after the Holocaust, thinks of himself as another person, someone utterly changed from the innocent boy who left Sighet, that person, that "corpse," undergoes a metamorphosis. Looking back, Eliezer realizes that he is no longer the corpse who was liberated from Buchenwald. He may be doomed to remember the look in the corpse's eyes, but he manages to keep himself separate from this empty shell of a man. Indeed, it is Eliezer's particular burden to remember the look in the corpse's eyes, because only by remembering and by bearing witness can the survivors of the Holocaust ensure that nothing like the Holocaust will ever happen again. But the memory of evil, as Wiesel realizes, and as Eliezer perhaps comes to realize in the process of separating himself from the corpse he has become as a result of his time in the concentration camps, can coexist with faith, both in God and in man.

Night does not end with optimism and a rosy message, but neither does it end as bleakly as many believe. What we are left with are questions—about God's and man's capacity for evil—but no true answers. *Night* does not try to answer these questions; perhaps this lack of answers is one of the reasons that the story ends with the liberation of Buchenwald. The moral responsibility for remembering the Holocaust, and for confronting these difficult moral and theological questions, falls directly upon us, the readers.

Important Quotations Explained

1. Never shall I forget that night, the first night in camp,
    which has turned my life into one long night, seven
    times cursed and seven times sealed. Never shall I
    forget that smoke. Never shall I forget the little faces
    of the children, whose bodies I saw turned into
    wreaths of smoke beneath a silent blue sky.
        Never shall I forget those flames which consumed
    my faith forever.
        Never shall I forget that nocturnal silence which
    deprived me, for all eternity, of the desire to live.
    Never shall I forget those moments which murdered
    my God and my soul and turned my dreams to dust.
    Never shall I forget these things, even if I am
    condemned to live as long as God Himself. Never.

This passage, from *Night*'s third section, occurs just after Eliezer
and his father realize they have survived the first selection at
Birkenau. It is perhaps *Night*'s most famous passage, notable
because it is one of the few moments in the memoir where Eliezer
breaks out of the continuous narrative stream with which he tells his
tale. As he reflects upon his horrendous first night in the concentration camp and its lasting effect on his life, Wiesel introduces the
theme of Eliezer's spiritual crisis and his loss of faith in God.

    In its form, this passage resembles two significant pieces of liter-
ature: Psalm 150, from the Bible, and French author Emile Zola's
1898 essay "J'accuse." Psalm 150, the final prayer in the book of
Psalms, is an ecstatic celebration of God. Each line begins, "Hallelujah," or "Praise God." Here, Wiesel constructs an inverse version
of that psalm, beginning each line with a negation—"Never"—that
replaces the affirmative "Hallelujah" of the original. Whereas
Psalm 150 praises God, this passage questions him. As such, both
the form and content of this passage reflect the inversion of Eliezer's
faith and the morality of the world around him. Everything he once
believed has been turned upside down, in the same way that this
passage's words invert both the form and content of Psalm 150.

Zola's essay "J'accuse" was a response to the Dreyfus Affair, an incident in which a Jewish army officer was unjustly convicted of treason, a judgment at least partially motivated by anti-Semitism. Zola responded by publishing an open letter in the Paris newspaper *L'Aurore*, denouncing the authorities who had covered up the injustice and perpetuated the persecution. Zola heightened the aggressive tone of the letter by repeatedly stressing the refrain "J'accuse" ("I accuse").

The similarities between Wiesel's passage and Zola's—the French words of the refrain, the anti-Semitic context, and the defiant tone—invite comparison between the two texts. Zola's piece was an impassioned accusation that decried injustice and anti-Semitism; Wiesel's passage is also an impassioned polemic, but its target is God Himself. Zola's "j'accuse" is directed at corrupt officials who have betrayed an innocent Jew; here, Eliezer's "jamais" ("never") is directed toward God. Carrying the comparison even further, Eliezer's statement depicts God as a corrupt official betraying the Jews. This is a shockingly bold statement for a Jewish boy to make and reflects the profound way in which his faith has been shaken. Furthermore, the fact that Zola's transitive verb ("I accuse") has been replaced by an objectless adverb ("never") reflects the prisoners' powerlessness to remedy their situation. Although Wiesel's passage is directed *toward* God, it is not directed *at* any specific being; since the prisoners are powerless to strike back, their anger cannot take the form of a direct confrontation.

Eliezer claims that his faith is utterly destroyed, yet at the same time says that he will never forget these things even if he "live[s] as long as God Himself." After completely denying the existence of God, he refers to God's existence in the final line. As mentioned before, Wiesel wrote elsewhere, "My anger rises up within faith and not outside it." Eliezer reflects this position, which is particularly visible throughout this passage. Despite saying he has lost all faith, it is clear that Eliezer is actually *struggling* with his faith and his God. Just as he is never able to forget the horror of "that night," he is never able to reject completely his heritage and his religion.

2. "Where is God? Where is He?" someone behind me
    asked. . .
    For more than half an hour [the child in the noose]
    stayed there, struggling between life and death, dying
    in slow agony under our eyes. And we had to look
    him full in the face. He was still alive when I passed in
    front of him. His tongue was still red, his eyes were
    not yet glazed.
    Behind me, I heard the same man asking:
    "Where is God now?"
    And I heard a voice within me answer him:
    "Where is He? Here He is—He is hanging here on
    this gallows. . . ."

This passage occurs at the end of the fourth section, as Eliezer witnesses the agonizingly slow death of the Dutch Oberkapo's *pipel*, a
young boy hanged for collaborating against the Nazis. This horrible
moment signifies the low point of Eliezer's faith in God. The death
of the child also symbolizes the death of Eliezer's own childhood
and innocence. The suffering Eliezer sees and experiences during the
Holocaust transforms his entire worldview. Before the war, he cannot imagine questioning his God. When asked by Moshe the Beadle
why he prays, Eliezer replies, "Why did I pray? What a strange question. Why did I live? Why did I breathe?" Observance and belief
were unquestioned parts of his core sense of identity, so once his
faith is irreparably shaken, he becomes a completely different person. Among other things, *Night* is a perverse coming-of-age story, in
which Eliezer's innocence is cruelly stripped from him.

QUOTATIONS

3. We were masters of nature, masters of the world. We
    had forgotten everything—death, fatigue, our natural
    needs. Stronger than cold or hunger, stronger than the
    shots and the desire to die, condemned and
    wandering, mere numbers, we were the only men
    on earth.
        At last, the morning star appeared in the gray sky.
    A trail of indeterminate light showed on the horizon.
    We were exhausted. We were without strength,
    without illusions.

This passage occurs in the sixth section of the book, toward the end
of the prisoners' horrible run from Buna. It succinctly describes the
prisoners' godless worldview, which holds survival to be the highest
principle and all other morality to be meaningless. In Jewish prayer,
God is often referred to as "Master of the Universe." At this point,
the prisoners have replaced God in that role; they themselves are the
masters of nature and the world. Eliezer's experiences have instilled
in him the despairing sense that he is alone in the world, a "mere
number," responsible only for his own survival.

By omitting a conjunction between "without strength" and
"without illusions" in the last sentence, Wiesel makes the relationship between the two concepts ambiguous. It is unclear whether the
ideas are complementary ("We were without strength because we
were without illusions") or unrelated ("We were without strength,
and also we were without illusions"). Using the former interpretation, the sentence implies that illusion—perhaps the illusion of
faith—can give one strength. As we see when he discusses the death
of Akiba Drumer, Eliezer acknowledges that faith gives a person a
sense of being and a reason to struggle. By this point in his experience, he is deeply cynical about faith; for him, it is a mere illusion, a
deluded belief in an omnipotent creator who doesn't exist. Along
similar lines, the phrase "condemned and wandering" references
the entire history of Jewish suffering, a history defined by exile and
exclusion. Despite his professed lack of faith, Eliezer is approaching
his struggle from within the context of Judaism, not from outside it.

QUOTATIONS

4. [Rabbi Eliahou's son] had felt that his father was growing weak, he had believed that the end was near and had sought this separation in order to get rid of the burden, to free himself from an encumbrance which could lessen his own chances of survival.

    I had done well to forget that. And I was glad that Rabbi Eliahou should continue to look for his beloved son.

    And, in spite of myself, a prayer rose in my heart, to that God in whom I no longer believed.

    My God, Lord of the Universe, give me strength never to do what Rabbi Eliahou's son has done.

This passage is found in the sixth section, during the respite from the march to Gleiwitz. First and most obviously, it emphasizes the centrality of the father-son relationship in Eliezer's life. As Eliezer expresses when discussing Akiba Drumer's despair, every victim of the Holocaust needed a reason to struggle, a reason to want to survive. For many, that reason was faith in God and the ultimate goodness of mankind. But since Eliezer has lost that faith, his relationship with his father is what keeps him struggling.

Eliezer's experience has taught him that the Nazis' cruelty distorts one's perspective and engenders cruelty among the prisoners. Self-preservation becomes the highest virtue in the world of the Holocaust and leads prisoners to commit horrendous crimes against one another. Eliezer fears that this loss of perspective will happen to him, that he will lose control over himself and turn against his father. In the concentration camps, Eliezer has learned that *any* human being, even himself, is capable of unimaginable cruelty.

Eliezer's prayer to God reflects the incomplete nature of his loss of faith. Because Eliezer senses his potential for weakness, he appeals to a greater power for help. He says he no longer believes in God, but he nevertheless turns to God when he doubts his ability to control himself. Eliezer no longer considers himself "master of nature, master of the world," as he did in the previous passage. Instead, he needs help controlling his base instincts.

QUOTATIONS

5. One day I was able to get up, after gathering all my strength. I wanted to see myself in the mirror hanging on the opposite wall. I had not seen myself since the ghetto.

    From the depths of the mirror, a corpse gazed back at me.

    The look in his eyes, as they stared into mine, has never left me.

This is the final passage of *Night,* Eliezer's final statement about the effect the Holocaust has had on him. As such, it reinforces the book's deliberately limited perspective. *Night* does not pretend to be a comprehensive survey of World War II experiences, nor does it try to explore the general experience of Jews in concentration camps. Instead, it focuses on one specific story—Eliezer's—to give the reader a detailed, personal account of suffering in the Holocaust. From a more traditional perspective, the ending feels incomplete. A historian or biographer would not be satisfied with this conclusion and would want to know what happened afterward—how Eliezer reunited with his family, what he did after the war, and so on. *Night* deliberately manipulates narrative conventions, ending where it does because it is meant to offer an intimate portrayal of Eliezer's wartime experiences, particularly of the cruelty and suffering he experiences in the concentration camps. Other material would distract from the intensity of the experience Wiesel is trying to convey.

    Eliezer implies that even though he has survived the war physically, he is essentially dead, his soul killed by the suffering he witnessed and endured. Yet, when Eliezer says, "the look in his eyes, as he stared into mine," he implies a separation between himself and the corpse. His language, too, indicates a fundamental separation between his sense of self and his identity as a Holocaust victim—as if he has become two distinct beings. The corpse-image reminds him how much he has suffered and how much of himself—his faith in God, his innocence, his faith in mankind, his father, his mother, his sister—has been killed in the camps. At the same time, he manages to separate himself from this empty shell. The image of the corpse will always stay with him, but he has found a sense of identity that will endure beyond the Holocaust. As dark as this passage is, its message is partially hopeful. Eliezer survives beyond the horrible suffering he endured by separating himself from it, casting it aside so he can remember, but not continue to feel, the horror.

KEY FACTS

FULL TITLE
Night

AUTHOR
Elie Wiesel

TYPE OF WORK
Literary memoir

GENRE
World War II and Holocaust autobiography

LANGUAGE
Wiesel first wrote a 900-page text in Yiddish titled *Un di Velt Hot Geshvign* (*And the World Remained Silent*). The work later evolved into the much-shorter French publication *La Nuit*, which was then translated into English as *Night*.

TIME AND PLACE WRITTEN
Mid-1950s, Paris. Wiesel began writing after a ten-year self-imposed vow of silence about the Holocaust.

DATE OF FIRST PUBLICATION
Un di Velt Hot Geshvign was first published in 1956 in Buenos Aires. *La Nuit* was published in France in 1958, and the English translation was published in 1960.

PUBLISHER
Unión Central Israelita Polaca (in Buenos Aires); Les Editions de Minuit (in France); Hill & Wang (in the United States)

NARRATOR
Eliezer (a slightly fictionalized version of Elie Wiesel)

POINT OF VIEW
Eliezer speaks in the first person and always relates the autobiographical events from his perspective.

TONE

Eliezer's perspective is limited to his own experience, and the tone of *Night* is therefore intensely personal, subjective, and intimate. *Night* is not meant to be an all-encompassing discourse on the experience of the Holocaust; instead, it depicts the extraordinarily personal and painful experiences of a single victim.

TENSE

Past

SETTING (TIME)

1941–1945, during World War II

SETTINGS (PLACE)

Eliezer's story begins in Sighet, Transylvania (now part of Romania; during Wiesel's childhood, part of Hungary). The book then follows his journey through several concentration camps in Europe: Auschwitz/Birkenau (in a part of modern-day Poland that had been annexed by Germany in 1939), Buna (a camp that was part of the Auschwitz complex), Gleiwitz (also in Poland but annexed by Germany), and Buchenwald (Germany).

PROTAGONIST

Eliezer

MAJOR CONFLICT

Eliezer's struggles with Nazi persecution, and with his own faith in God and in humanity

RISING ACTION

Eliezer's journey through the various concentration camps and the subsequent deterioration of his father and himself

CLIMAX

The death of Eliezer's father

FALLING ACTION

The liberation of the concentration camps, the time spent in silence between Eliezer's liberation and Elie Wiesel's decision to write about his experience, referred to in the memoir when Eliezer jumps ahead to events that happened after the Holocaust

THEMES
Eliezer's struggle to maintain faith in a benevolent God; silence; inhumanity toward other humans; the importance of father-son bonds

MOTIFS
Tradition, religious observance

SYMBOLS
Night, fire

FORESHADOWING
Night does not operate like a novel, using foreshadowing to hint at surprises to come. The pall of tragedy hangs over the entire novel, however. Even as early as the work's dedication, "In memory of my parents and my little sister, Tzipora," Wiesel makes it evident that Eliezer will be the only significant character in the book who survives the war. As readers, we are not surprised by their inevitable deaths; instead, Wiesel's narrative shocks and stuns us with the details of the cruelty that the prisoners experience.

STUDY QUESTIONS & ESSAY TOPICS

STUDY QUESTIONS

1. *In his 1996 memoir* All Rivers Run to the Sea, *Elie Wiesel writes, in reference to the responsibility of the Holocaust survivor, "To be silent is impossible, to speak forbidden." What do you think Wiesel means? How does he resolve or circumvent this paradox?*

Those who did not live through the Holocaust, it is fair to say, cannot begin to understand what it was like; those who did cannot begin to describe it. To speak of the concentration camps is to fail to convey the depth of the evil, and any failure is disrespectful to the memories of those who died in the Holocaust. Speech, therefore, may seem forbidden, because it necessarily fails to express the truth of the Holocaust.

Yet, if nobody speaks of the Holocaust, those who died will go forgotten. It has become a commonplace among AIDS activists to use a slogan equating silence with death; similarly, it is the very real fear of many Holocaust survivors that a failure to speak about what happened during the Holocaust could lead to a possible recurrence of the same evil. Silence, it is sometimes said, gives a posthumous victory to Hitler, because it erases the memory of the atrocities that were committed at his command.

Night is the expression of an author, and a narrator, caught between silence and speech. Eliezer often maintains something of a clinical detachment when describing the horrors of the camps. He avoids becoming gruesome or ever describing in precise detail the extent of his suffering. He refuses to describe a person in agony, content to mention the fact of agony's existence. He withdraws from the subject, sensing that approaching it too closely would be sacrilege. Wiesel carefully avoids melodrama and intense scrutiny of the events. relating the facts of his experiences. *Night* is moving not because of Wiesel's passionate prose, but because of his reticence. "The secret of truth," Wiesel writes elsewhere, "lies in silence."

2.   *Does Wiesel believe that God is dead? Does the narrator, Eliezer?*

In *Night,* Eliezer says that the Holocaust "murdered his God," and he often expresses the belief that God could not exist and permit the existence of the Holocaust. Elie Wiesel and Eliezer are not exactly the same, but Eliezer expresses, in most cases, the emotions that Wiesel felt at the time of the Holocaust. It is fair to say that *Night* contains a profound skepticism about God's existence. Yet Eliezer is not enlightened by his rejection of God; instead, he is reduced to the shell of a person. Likewise, Akiba Drumer, upon abandoning his faith, loses his will to live. Wiesel seems to be suggesting that the events of the Holocaust prove that faith *is* a necessary element in human survival, because it preserves man, whether or not it is based in reality. Faith, Wiesel seems to say, enables hope, and it is always necessary for the prisoners to maintain hope, in order for them to maintain life.

Even when Eliezer claims to abandon God as an abstract idea, he remains incapable of abandoning his attachment to God as an everyday part of his life. He continues to pray to God—he prays not to become as cruel as Rabbi Eliahou's son, for instance—and his vocabulary still reflects a kernel of faith in God. It seems that Eliezer, at his core, still maintains a kind of belief in God. Wiesel remarks in *All Rivers Run to the Sea,* "Theorists of the idea that 'God is Dead' have used my words unfairly as justification of their rejection of faith. But if Nietzsche could cry out . . . that God is dead, the Jew in me cannot. I have never renounced my faith in God."

3. *What role does chance play in Eliezer's survival of the Holocaust? What role does choice play? Do your answers to these questions have any implications regarding the extent of control that a person has over his or her life?*

Wiesel makes a distinction between the Holocaust victims' control over their fate and their control over their actions. He believes man *does* have control over his moral choices, even when faced with the extreme circumstances of the Holocaust. Although he empathizes with the Jews who behave brutally, killing each other over crusts of bread in their fight to survive, he does not condone their behavior. At the same time, one senses that Eliezer, and Wiesel, feel there are definite limits to the victims' control over their fate. It would be disrespectful to those who died for Eliezer—or Wiesel himself—to claim any credit for surviving.

For this reason, *Night* chronicles and emphasizes the set of lucky circumstances that led to the survival of one among many. The memoir is filled with bizarre coincidences. Years after the Holocaust, Eliezer randomly meets the woman who gave him comfort in Buna. In Gleiwitz, Eliezer once again meets Juliek. Eliezer's teacher, Moshe the Beadle, somehow escapes the Nazis and returns to Sighet to convey to the town an unheeded warning. Perhaps the most bizarre coincidence of all is Eliezer's survival. He is fortunate enough, on his arrival in Birkenau, to meet a man who tells him to lie about his age. Despite Eliezer's small size, he does not succumb to cold or exhaustion and is not chosen in any of the selections, though many who are healthier than he is are sent to the gas chambers.

SUGGESTED ESSAY TOPICS

1. One of the most tragic themes in *Night* is Eliezer's discovery of the way that atrocities and cruel treatment can make good people into brutes. Does he himself escape this fate?

2. *Night* is essentially Elie Wiesel's memoir about his experiences in the Holocaust. Yet, there are minor differences between Wiesel's own experiences and those of *Night*'s narrator, Eliezer. Why might that be? Must a memoir be absolutely factual?

3. Elie Wiesel won the Nobel Peace Prize in 1986 for his championing of human rights around the world. How might his advocacy for human rights have grown out of his Holocaust experiences? What are the positive lessons of the Holocaust that Wiesel hints at in *Night*?

4. In the midst of the dying men in Gleiwitz, the violinist Juliek plays a fragment of music written by the German composer Beethoven. Before and after the Holocaust, many people wondered how the Germans, cultured Europeans, could commit such barbaric acts. Does Wiesel suggest any rationale behind the Holocaust in *Night*? Does he speculate as to the motives of the perpetrators? What, for Wiesel, are those motives, if they exist?

5. The Rabbi of Kotzk, a European village later destroyed in the Holocaust, is famous for being bold enough to challenge God: "Our Father, our King," he said, "I shall continue to call You Father until You become our Father." For Wiesel, is there a purpose to faith even without the existence or justice of God? What do you believe?

6. It is possible to look at *Night* as the story of Eliezer's loss of innocence. It might be argued, too, that innocence is impossible after the Holocaust. Is this true? Is it tragic, or is innocence an impediment to survival, as when the Jews are too innocent to believe that Hitler really means to kill them?

Review & Resources

Quiz

1. What town do Eliezer and his family come from?

    A. Gleiwitz
    B. Sighet
    C. Haifa
    D. Budapest

2. What specifically does Eliezer recruit Moshe the Beadle to teach him?

    A. The Cabbala
    B. The Talmud
    C. The Torah
    D. The Haftorah

3. What is Eliezer's oldest sister's name?

    A. Béa
    B. Hilda
    C. Tzipora
    D. Esther

4. Upon his return to the village, What does Moshe the Beadle try to do?

    A. Break into Eliezer's home
    B. Spy for the Nazis
    C. Become a Rabbi
    D. Warn the villagers about the Nazi threat

5. After being evacuated from their original homes, where are the Jews of Sighet first sent?

    A. To Auschwitz/Birkenau
    B. To a ghetto within Sighet
    C. To Czechoslovakia
    D. To Buna

6. On what day is Eliezer's family deported from Sighet?

    A. Rosh Hashanah, the Jewish New Year
    B. Yom Kippur, the Day of Atonement
    C. The first day of Passover, the commemoration of the Exodus from Egypt
    D. The Sabbath, the day of rest

7. On the train from Sighet, of what does Madame Schächter has visions?

    A. A gas chamber
    B. Israel
    C. A furnace
    D. Angels of liberation

8. What do several men on the train do when they are unable to endure Madame Schächter's screaming?

    A. Stuff their ears with cotton
    B. Beat her senseless
    C. Jump off the train
    D. Persuade her son to keep her quiet

9. From whom is Eliezer separated at Birkenau?

    A. His mother and three sisters
    B. His father
    C. Both his parents
    D. His entire family

10. During the first selection at Birkenau, what do Eliezer and his father, respectively, pretend their ages are?

    A. Fifteen and fifty
    B. Fifteen and forty
    C. Eighteen and forty
    D. Eighteen and fifty

11. Who is the infamous Nazi doctor presiding over the Auschwitz arrivals?

    A. Dr. Mankle
    B. Dr. Mengele
    C. Dr. Menglein
    D. Dr. Maunklietz

12. What is the Kaddish?

    A. The Jewish prayer for the dead
    B. A leader of the Jewish community
    C. The Hebrew translation of "The Holocaust"
    D. The book of Jewish mysticism

13. In Birkenau, who beats Eliezer's father?

    A. Meir Katz
    B. A gypsy Kapo
    C. An S.S. guard
    D. A horde of prisoners

14. At Auschwitz, wh recognizes Eliezer and his father?

    A. Their relative from Antwerp, named Stein
    B. A French Jewish woman posing as an Aryan
    C. Their rabbi from Sighet
    D. An old customer of Eliezer's father

15. At Buna, with whom is Eliezer placed in a block?

    A. Electricians
    B. Masons
    C. Farmers
    D. Musicians

16. What is Idek?

    A. Eliezer's Kapo in the electrical equipment warehouse
    B. A violinist who befriends Eliezer
    C. Yosi's brother
    D. An old Jewish mystic

17. To whom does Eliezer lose the gold crown on his tooth?

    A. Franek
    B. Idek
    C. Akiba Drumer
    D. A Jewish dentist from Czechoslovakia

18. What do the Gestapo do after an instance of sabotage
    at Buna?

    A. Arrest Eliezer
    B. Torture Eliezer's father
    C. Hang a young child
    D. Close down Buna

19. After Akiba Drumer's death, what do Eliezer and the other
    prisoners do?

    A. Decorate his grave
    B. Forget to say the prayer for the dead
    C. Rebel against the Nazis
    D. Secretly light memorial candles in his honor

20. In January 1945, what sort of infection does
    Eliezer contract?

    A. Mouth
    B. Thumb
    C. Stomach
    D. Foot

21. In the concentration camp hospital, Eliezer's neighbor remarks he has lost faith in everything except what?

    A. God
    B. Death
    C. Hitler
    D. Eliezer

22. During the long run after Buna, what does Eliezer say was the only thing that kept him from giving up?

    A. His faith in God
    B. His desire for justice
    C. His father's presence
    D. A sense of pride

23. In the shed, taking a brief break from the run, what does Eliezer pray for?

    A. For the dead
    B. For an end to the war
    C. For the strength to never abandon his father for his own benefit
    D. For a quick end to their long journey

24. In the barracks at Gleiwitz, what does Eliezer hear?

    A. His mother's voice
    B. The quiet prayers of all the Jewish prisoners
    C. Rabbi Eliahou's son mercilessly berating his father
    D. Juliek playing Beethoven on the violin

25. Where does Eliezer's father die?

    A. Gleiwitz
    B. Buchenwald
    C. Birkenau
    D. Buna

GLOSSARY OF RELEVANT TERMS

Adam and Eve The first two human beings created by God. Adam and Eve disobeyed God by eating fruit that he had forbidden; as punishment, God expelled them from the Garden of Eden.

Angel of Death A prominent character in Jewish folk tradition. In the Bible, angels appeared only as personifications of divine will, but in postbiblical literature and tradition, they gradually began to be seen as somewhat independent supernatural beings. The Angel of Death was a particularly fearsome angel who would stand at the bedside of the sick and, using his knife, take their life. A series of interesting rituals evolved concerning the Angel of Death, including the practice of changing one's name during extreme illness in an attempt to fool the Angel and the practice of discarding all water in a room after a death (due to the belief that, after a death, the Angel cleaned his knife in whatever water was near the deathbed). In *Night,* Eliezer's reference to the Angel of Death suggests the deep Jewish folk tradition of his upbringing. Historically, Dr. Mengele was nicknamed "The Angel of Death."

Baruch In traditional observance, Jews are required to give thanks constantly to God for the world around them, and there are a multitude of specific prayers tailored for specific occasions of thanksgiving. In general, these prayers begin with a phrase known as "baruch," the text of which translates roughly to "Blessed Art Thou, Lord our God, Ruler of the Universe." It is this phrase with which Eliezer begins his sarcastic prayer during his Rosh Hashanah observance in 1944. He cynically twists a traditional observance of thanks into a statement about how little gratitude he has toward God, reflecting his loss of faith.

Beadle   Also called a Shammash (meaning "servant") in
Hebrew, the beadle is the Jewish synagogue's
equivalent of the church sexton; he prepares the temple
for services and performs daily maintenance.

"Blessed Art Thou" See Baruch.

Cabbala   Most often spelled "Kabbalah" or "Cabala" (but
spelled "Cabbala" in *Night*), Cabbala refers to the
tradition of Jewish mysticism, particularly the
mysticism codified in the Zohar. But because "the
Cabbala" refers to not a single thing but a tradition (in
fact, the Hebrew translation of "Cabbala" is "that
which is received," i.e., a tradition), it is a term that
encompasses a broad range of beliefs and practices,
and is difficult to reduce to a single definition.
Generally speaking, Cabbalistic thought teaches that
the mysteries of God are all around us, always within
us, and that the goal of religious study is to approach
these mysteries and, in doing so, to better understand
the mystical secrets of divine nature and of the world
around us.

Captivity of Babylon More commonly known as the
"Babylonian Exile," the Captivity of Babylon refers to
a period of time (587 to 536 B.C.) after Israel was
conquered by King Nebuchadnezzar and the Jews were
imprisoned in Nebuchadnezzar's kingdom of
Babylonia. Exile and captivity are recurring themes
throughout Jewish tradition, so, to many people, the
Holocaust was a horrible modern manifestation of a
phenomenon that has been going on for thousands of
years: the persecution, imprisonment, and relocation of
the Jewish people.

Destruction of the Temple This phrase is a reference to the
destruction of the sacred temple on Mount Moriah in
Jerusalem, one of the most significant tragedies in
Jewish history. The temple had originally been built by
King Solomon, who had been instructed by his father,
King David. After its completion around 1000 B.C., the

temple became the holiest place in Israel. In 587 B.C., the temple was destroyed by Nebuchadnezzar, the king of Babylon, marking the beginning of the first exile from Israel (see Captivity of Babylon, The). After the Babylonian Exile, Jerusalem experienced a Jewish restoration, resulting in the building of the Second Temple. This Temple was destroyed by the Romans in 700 A.D., on the same day of the year—the ninth of Av in the Jewish calendar—that the First Temple was destroyed. Some have argued that this second destruction was actually the greater trauma to the nation of Israel, because it marked the beginning of the Jewish Diaspora, the scattering of Jews throughout the world.

End of the World Although some have argued that there are a few references to the Apocalypse within the Jewish Bible, the concept of the end of the world is largely a postbiblical phenomenon. In Jewish tradition, this end will include a regathering of the scattered Jewish Diaspora, the last great conflict between forces of good and evil, a Day of Judgment, the coming of the Messiah, the resurrection of the dead, and the reestablishment of paradise on Earth. But because this concept is largely part of nonliturgical Jewish folk tradition, specifics vary widely. During the Holocaust, some mystical Jews interpreted the immense suffering as a sign that the end of the world was close at hand, that the ultimate evil had risen and soon the Messiah would come to defeat it. This is the viewpoint alluded to by the Hasid Hersch Genud at the end of the third section.

Eternal Flame All Jewish temples have a light that is always kept on, either an electrified bulb or a flame that is always lit. It is a symbolic reference to the Eternal Flame prescribed in the Bible (Exodus 27:20–21 and Leviticus 24:2) that was kept burning in the First Temple. In the words of one scholar, this Eternal Flame represents, "among other things, the eternal watchfulness and providence of God over His people."

In *Night,* however, flame and fire symbolize Nazi power and cruelty. Thus, the use of fire in the book reflects Eliezer's loss of faith. What was once a symbol of God's munificence is now a symbol of the evil that Eliezer sees in the world.

Faith   Throughout *Night,* Eliezer struggles with his faith in God. He notes of Akiba Drumer that "as soon as he felt the first cracks forming in his faith, he had lost his reason for struggling and had begun to die." The idea of faith is central to the book, and it is important to understand the specifically Jewish meaning of the term. In traditional Judaism, faith is of less importance than religious observance. One Talmudic passage (see Talmud) has God say, "Would that they abandoned Me, but observed my commandments—since the light thereof would turn them again to me." In other words, in Judaism, actions are much more important than words or thoughts (although, it should be noted, words and thoughts also carry significant weight).

This privileging of actions over thoughts explains some of Eliezer's perplexing behavior. For example, though Eliezer professes he has lost his faith in God, he feels conflicted about the Yom Kippur fast. In the context of traditional Jewish conceptions of faith, Eliezer's loss of faith reflects an ongoing religious struggle and is not a total act of sacrilege. But in the context of Hasidism, the type of Judaism practiced by Eliezer, the loss of faith in God is a more serious matter. As a mystical movement, Hasidism stresses the presence of God in oneself and throughout the material world. As such, faith in God is of utmost importance to Hasidic conceptions of oneself and the daily process of living. In this context, Eliezer's loss of faith reflects a profound conflict with his fundamental religious and cultural values.

Fasting   In Judaism, as in many other religions, fasting (abstaining from eating or drinking) is an exercise in penitence. It is most often discussed in the context of Yom Kippur.

REVIEW & RESOURCES

"Gave Thanks to God" See Baruch.

Haifa   A popular port city in northern Israel, located on the Mediterranean.

Hasidism A mystical movement within Judaism, controversial since it originated in the eighteenth century in Poland. The movement was founded by the charismatic leader Israel ben Elizier, better known as the Baal Shem Tov (or the Besht). Throughout the seventeenth century, the substantial Polish Jewish community experienced many hardships: crippling poverty, horrible persecution by Cossacks, and deception by an infamous false Messiah. All these factors, particularly the last, created an environment of spiritual crisis and questioning of faith.

When the Besht appeared at the turn of the century with a fairly radical new expression of Judaism, he became known as a healer with almost magical powers. He preached a mystical interpretation of Judaism, stressing joy and divine transportation. Hasidic services featured (and continue to feature) song, dance, rejoicing, and ecstatic rapture during prayer. It is said that the Besht's body, and often the entire building, would shake uncontrollably during worship. In an environment of spiritual crisis, this new ecstatic, mystical form of Judaism quickly gained popularity and helped many Jews rediscover their faith. It soon spread throughout Eastern Europe and remains a significant movement within Judaism, particularly in Europe and America.

Elie Wiesel was raised in a Hasidic community, and in *Night* this religious movement plays a significant role in Eliezer's story. The work never specifically introduces the tenets of Hasidic belief, but they are nonetheless very important to understanding the journey of faith and doubt experienced by Eliezer. First and foremost, Hasidism is a mystical movement, and as such it stresses the omnipresence of God, even more so than traditional Judaism. Like many mystical movements, Hasidism teaches that God is everywhere, in everything, around us all the time, and that even that even our smallest actions are affected by—and affect— the divine presence. Because he was raised to feel that God was everywhere, all the time, when Eliezer experiences the horrors of the camps his crisis of faith is all the more profound. Hasidism teaches that "there is no place empty of Him," yet Eliezer cannot believe that God is in the bloody, fiery concentration camps.

Along similar lines, Hasidism stresses a connection between the heavenly and terrestrial spheres. According to Hasidic beliefs, everything on Earth is an "emanation" or reflection of the divine world. Thus, when Eliezer sees such tragedy and ugliness, it becomes hard for him to accept that God is pure and good. Hasidism also stresses a fundamental joy in life and religion. During the horrors of the Holocaust, it is hard for Eliezer to feel that life and faith contain any joy at all. He sees people, both captors and prisoners, committing the most unimaginable acts of cruelty, and comes to believe that cruelty, not joy and kindness, is the fundament of human nature.

Jerusalem The capital of Israel in the era of King David. Jerusalem became the holiest of Jewish cities, and Jewish synagogues throughout the world are aligned so that the Torah (the scroll containing the Old Testament of the Bible) faces Jerusalem. After the Jewish exile from Israel and subsequent Diaspora, Jerusalem became a city of great significance for Christianity, and then for Islam. Today, Jerusalem's ownership and identity is hotly contested.

Jewish Mysticism See Cabbala.

Job The most famous sufferer in the Bible. In the Book of Job, Satan challenges God, saying that even the most faithful believers would lose faith in God if afflicted with adversity. God decides to test his faithful servant Job by torturing the poor shepherd and farmer with all manner of tragedy. Job maintains his faith through these trials, and he is eventually rewarded with fortune, family, and health. Job's experience contrasts sharply with Eliezer's: Eliezer feels that his suffering is needless and purposeless, and it causes him to doubt God. Whereas Job keeps his faith, Eliezer loses his.

Kaddish   The Jewish prayer of mourning for the dead. Mourning is an important tradition for Jews, since in Maimonides' code of law (see Maimonides) it is written, "Whoever does not mourn as the sages instructed is cruel." What is unusual about the *Kaddish,* as a prayer for the dead, is that it does not mention death, the afterlife, or sorrow at all. The bulk of the prayer is a celebration of God's glory, and it concludes with a prayer for peace. In *Night,* Eliezer's feelings about *Kaddish* serve as an example of his growing doubts about Jewish tradition. Amid all the suffering and sorrow, he disdains a prayer for the dead that exalts God and prays for peace, because he feels that God has abandoned the sufferers and that peace is completely unattainable.

Maimonides Born Moses ben Maimon, Maimonides (also called Rambam) lived from 1135 to 1204 and is generally considered the greatest Jewish philosopher. He authored numerous works of biblical, Talmudic (see Talmud), and philosophical scholarship. Outside of Jewish tradition, his most famous work is *The Guide for the Perplexed,* in which he tries to reconcile Judaism and Aristotelian philosophy.

Messiah   In the words of *The Encyclopedia of the Jewish Religion,* the Messiah is the "long-awaited, Divinely chosen king of the Davidic line who would rule over a new golden age" after the end of the world. Although Christian tradition holds that Jesus Christ was this Messiah, Jews believe that the Messiah has yet to arrive. In certain Jewish circles, there is the belief that suffering and repentance hasten the coming of this Messiah, hence Eliezer's comment that he would fast "in order to hasten the coming of the Messiah."

Noah   A descendant of Adam and Eve. God flooded the earth to kill humanity on account of its wicked ways, but he spared Noah and his family, who survived by boarding the famous ark.

Numerology   In general, numerology is the mystical study of numbers. Practitioners of numerology find hidden or supernatural significance in numbers or patterns. In Judaism, discussion of numerology refers specifically to the practice of Gematria. In Hebrew, there are no unique characters for numbers; instead, all the letters of the alphabet have numerical values and are used in place of a separate numerical system. As a result, every Hebrew word can also be read as a number (often several different numbers, depending on parsing and interpretation). Gematria is the study of Scriptural passages as numbers; those who practice it use numerology to uncover hidden or mystical meanings in the text. It is a practice particularly associated with Hasidism, explaining Akiba Drumer's fondness for it in *Night*.

Palestine   It is difficult to give a definition of Palestine, other than to say it is a long-contested geographical area in the Middle East. For Jews, it is the area thought to be roughly analogous with the ancient country of Israel. At the time of Eliezer's story, Palestine was a geographical area controlled by Britain, not an autonomous country. Motivated in part by the Zionist movement (see Zionism), many Jews lived there (although many Jews were already living there prior to the advent of Zionism in 1898) and hoped to transform the area into an autonomous Jewish state. Today, the area is officially the modern state of Israel, but Israel's claim to the land remains contested by Palestinians and other Arab nations.

Passover   An important, eight-day Jewish holiday that commemorates the Jews' liberation from bondage in Egypt. The holiday's name refers to the biblical story of God's sparing, or passing over, the Jewish families during the final plague He visited upon the Egyptians— the killing of the first-born child.

Pentecost   Also called the "Feast of Weeks," Pentecost originated as the festival celebrating the conclusion of the grain harvest but evolved into a celebration of God's revelation to Moses on Mount Sinai, when God gave Moses the Torah (the first five books of the Old Testament).

Phylacteries   Two small leather boxes containing specific passages from the Bible (Exodus 13:1, Exodus 13:11, Deuteronomy 6:4–9, and Deuteronomy 11:13–21) written on parchment. As part of the traditional morning prayer ritual, Jews bind these boxes with thin leather straps to the head and left arm.

Rabbi   The Jewish equivalent of a priest, a rabbi is officially defined as a person "qualified to give decisions of Jewish law." Because Jews in Europe often lived in exclusively Jewish communities, the rabbi often functioned as a general community leader as well as a religious leader.

Rosh Hashanah   Literally "The Head of the Year," Rosh Hashanah marks the Jewish New Year. Jewish tradition has its own calendar and system of numbering years, and Rosh Hashanah occurs in the fall, unlike the winter New Year of the Gregorian calendar. In 1944, Jews would have been celebrating the coming of the new year 5705. It is significant that Eliezer never mentions this number and refers to the years in Gregorian terms; it reflects the distance that has grown between him and his tradition.

Sabbath   The weekly day of rest, observed from sundown Friday through sundown Saturday. This day of observation commemorates the seventh day of creation in the Bible ("God blessed the seventh day, and sanctified it: because that in it he had rested from all his work which God created and made," Genesis 2:3 [King James version]). It is a solemn day of prayer and observance during which all labor is forbidden. The fact that the Nazis expelled Eliezer and his family on the Sabbath represents their disrespect for and profaning of the Jewish religion.

Satan   The Jewish conception of Satan is very different from the modern Christian conception of a devil lording over Hell. The word "satan" occurs frequently in the Old Testament, meaning "adversary," and most often refers to specific human beings. Yet, in a few instances, this "adversary" is clearly an evil spirit of significant power (as, for example, in the Book of Job). Nevertheless, in Judaism, "Satan" is not so much a specific evil being as a more general concept of the spirit of evil in the world. When Akiba Drumer evokes "Satan," he is referring to the Jewish conception of the word.

"Saturday, the Day of Rest" See Sabbath.

Shaving Head Jewish law contains strict regulations about cutting one's hair and facial hair. Razors are not permitted, and beards and earlocks are often considered sources of pride and commitment to tradition. Thus, the Nazi practice of shaving the prisoners' heads functioned as a means of humiliation and a denigration of Jewish tradition.

Sodom   An infamous sin-filled city that God destroys in Genesis 19, along with the evil city of Gomorrah. Sodom is a symbol of wickedness, and its destruction a symbol of God's righteous wrath.

Spanish Inquisition Among other things, an example of the historical persecution of the Jews (as well as the persecution of others with differing religious beliefs). From 1478 to 1834, Spanish officials conducted an extended persecution of non-Catholics (whom they deemed heretics) throughout Spain, Portugal, and associated overseas colonies. Jews were placed in an awkward situation, because the Inquisition only persecuted Christians who held heretical (for their purposes, non-Catholic) views. Theoretically, Jews, having never been Christians, could not be harmed. But in the anti-Semitic climate of the era, many Jews felt forced to convert to Christianity while secretly maintaining Jewish beliefs. If their treachery was discovered, the covert Jews were burned at the stake. *Night* recapitulates this seemingly hopeless situation.

Star of David Two triangles linked into a six-pointed star, the traditional symbol of the Jewish people. Its origins are obscure, and it only became the representative Jewish symbol sometime in the seventeenth century. During World War II, Nazi laws forced Jews in German-controlled areas to wear yellow Stars of David in order to identify themselves as Jewish.

Synagogue A Jewish house of worship.

Talmud Literally meaning "teaching," the Talmud is a distinctly Jewish religious text. The Talmud is a holy book, but it is not presumed to be the word of God, as is the Torah (the Old Testament of the Bible). It is a lengthy compilation of scholarly dissertations and arguments about Jewish law and biblical interpretation, compiled and written down between 200 and 500 A.D. The Talmud reflects the importance of scholarship, argument, and discussion in Jewish tradition.

Tattooing Leviticus 19:28 reads, "Ye shall not make any cuttings in your flesh for the dead, nor print any marks upon you" (King James version). Judaism has always interpreted this passage as a strict ban on tattooing. Thus, Nazi tattooing of concentration camp inmates served not only to dehumanize the prisoners but also to demoralize them and strip them of their religion and tradition. See Shaving Heads.

Waters of Jordan The largest river in Israel, stretching from the foot of Mount Hermon through the Sea of Galilee to the Dead Sea. It figures prominently in several biblical stories, particularly a miraculous crossing in Joshua (3:15–17) that marked the beginning of the conquest of Canaan. It has remained a prominent symbol throughout Jewish folklore.

Yellow Star See Star of David.

Yom Kippur For ten days after the Jewish New Year (Rosh Hashanah), Jews observe a solemn period of penitence in which they reflect on their sins and ask forgiveness. These so-called Days of Awe culminate in Yom Kippur, the most solemn of all Jewish holidays. Worshippers pray throughout the entire day, asking forgiveness for sins, and, as a sign of repentance and purification, undergo a twenty-five-hour fast, neither eating nor drinking. As shown in *Night,* many Jewish concentration camp prisoners were conflicted over whether to observe the religious injunction when they were already enduring such hardship. The fact that the Nazis hold a selection around Yom Kippur is a cruel irony, because during the Days of Awe, God supposedly chooses who shall live during the coming year and who shall die. The fact that the Nazis make this decision for the prisoners shows that Hitler's cruelty has replaced divine power for the prisoners. God has seemingly abandoned them, and the Nazis hold ultimate power.

Zionism   The political movement advocating the creation and support of a Jewish state in Israel and the return of Jews to Israel. Founded in 1897 by Theodor Herzl, the movement takes its name from Zion, the site of the first temple (see Destruction of the Temple). At the time of World War II, the modern state of Israel had not yet been established; Zionism then referred to the political movement to establish this state in Palestine.

Zohar   The central text of Cabbalistic knowledge (aside from the Bible), the Zohar is a compendium of mystic discourses dating, in written form, from the late thirteenth century.

SUGGESTIONS FOR FURTHER READING

CARGAS, HARRY JAMES, ed. *Telling the Tale: A Tribute to Elie Wiesel*. Saint Louis: Time Being Books, 1993.

DAWIDOWICZ, LUCY S. *The War Against the Jews: 1933–1945*. New York: Holt, Rinehart and Winston, 1975.

FINE, ELLEN S. *Legacy of* NIGHT: *The Literary Universe of Elie Wiesel*. Albany: State University of New York Press, 1982.

GREENBERG, IRVING, and ALVIN H. ROSENFELD, eds. *Confronting the Holocaust: The Impact of Elie Wiesel*. Bloomington: Indiana University Press, 1978.

SIBELMAN, SIMON P. *Silence in the Novels of Elie Wiesel*. New York: St. Martin's Press, 1995.

WERBLOWSKY, R. J., and GEOFFREY WIGODER, eds. *The Encyclopedia of the Jewish Religion*. New York: Holt, Rinehart and Winston, 1965.

WIESEL, ELIE. *All Rivers Run to the Sea*. New York: Knopf, 1996.

———. *Messengers of God*. New York: Random House, 1975.

WIESELTIER, LEON. *Kaddish*. New York: Random House, 1998.

YOUNG, JAMES E. *Writing and Rewriting the Holocaust*. Bloomington: Indiana University Press, 1988.

REVIEW & RESOURCES

A Note on the Type

The typeface used in SparkNotes study guides is Sabon, created by master typographer Jan Tschichold in 1964. Tschichold revolutionized the field of graphic design twice: first with his use of asymmetrical layouts and sanserif type in the 1930s when he was affiliated with the Bauhaus, then by abandoning assymetry and calling for a return to the classic ideals of design. Sabon, his only extant typeface, is emblematic of his latter program: Tschichold's design is a recreation of the types made by Claude Garamond, the great French typographer of the Renaissance, and his contemporary Robert Granjon. Fittingly, it is named for Garamond's apprentice, Jacques Sabon.